# WEST HIGHLAND
# WHITE TERRIER

DEBRA M. ELDREDGE, DVM

## West Highland White Terrier

Editor: Stephanie Fornino
Indexer: Sonja Armstrong
Designer: Patricia Escabi
Series Designer: Mary Ann Kahn

TFH Publications®
President/CEO: Glen S. Axelrod
Executive Vice President: Mark E. Johnson
Publisher: Christopher T. Reggio
Production Manager: Kathy Bontz

TFH Publications, Inc.®
One TFH Plaza
Third and Union Avenues
Neptune City, NJ 07753

Discovery Communications, Inc. Book Development Team: Marjorie Kaplan, President and General Manager, Animal Planet Media / Kelly Day, EVP and General Manager, Discovery Commerce / Elizabeth Bakacs, Vice President, Licensing and Creative / JP Stoops, Director, Licensing / Bridget Stoyko, Associate Art Director

Printed and bound in China

12 13 14 15 16 17    1 3 5 7 9 8 6 4 2

Library of Congress Cataloging-in-Publication Data
Eldredge, Debra.

West highland white terrier / Debra M. Eldredge.
    p. cm. -- (Dogs 101)
Includes index.
ISBN 978-0-7938-3726-7 (alk. paper)
1. West Highland white terrier. I. Title.
SF429.W4.E57 2012

636.755--dc23
                                    2011017783

*The Leader In Responsible Animal Care for Over 50 Years!®*
www.tfh.com

# CONTENTS

**1** ORIGINS OF YOUR WEST HIGHLAND WHITE TERRIER . . . . . . . . . . . 4

**2** CHARACTERISTICS OF YOUR WEST HIGHLAND WHITE TERRIER . . 16

**3** SUPPLIES FOR YOUR WEST HIGHLAND WHITE TERRIER . . . . . . . . 30

**4** FEEDING YOUR WEST HIGHLAND WHITE TERRIER . . . . . . . . . . . . . 42

**5** GROOMING YOUR WEST HIGHLAND WHITE TERRIER . . . . . . . . . . 56

**6** HEALTH OF YOUR WEST HIGHLAND WHITE TERRIER . . . . . . . . . . . 70

**7** TRAINING YOUR WEST HIGHLAND WHITE TERRIER . . . . . . . . . . . 90

**8** SOLVING PROBLEMS WITH YOUR WEST HIGHLAND WHITE
TERRIER . . . . . . . . . . . . . . . . . . . . . . . . . . . . . . . . . . . . . . . . . . . . . . . . . . 106

**9** ACTIVITIES WITH YOUR WEST HIGHLAND WHITE TERRIER . . . . . 120

RESOURCES . . . . . . . . . . . . . . . . . . . . . . . . . . . . . . . . . . . . . . . . . . . . . . . . 134

INDEX . . . . . . . . . . . . . . . . . . . . . . . . . . . . . . . . . . . . . . . . . . . . . . . . . . . . . 137

# ORIGINS OF YOUR WEST HIGHLAND WHITE TERRIER

Depending on the day, your Westie may seem like an angel dropped down from heaven, but in reality his origins are much earthier! Westies are hardy terriers designed and bred to handle rough conditions as well as be delightful companions.

## THE HISTORY OF THE DOG

Many experts believe that dogs split off from their wolf cousins about 100,000 years ago. The dog, *Canis familiaris*, has 78 chromosomes, just as wolves and coyotes do, so they can still interbreed. However, the dog genome contains within it some of the most "plastic" genes known; for a single gene, dogs have a huge number of variable expressions. Within the species known as dog, we have examples ranging from Chihuahuas to Irish Wolfhounds, with everything—including Westies—in between! No other species has such wide genetic variation.

Dogs have been companions of humankind for thousands of years. The start of the domestication process may have been as long as 30,000 years ago. The earliest burials showing human and dog bones together come from Germany about 14,000 years ago. A burial site from Iraq that is 12,000 years old shows a human cradling a puppy. Early indications of dog domestication show up in China from about 7000 to 5800 BCE. In the United States, combined burials from 11,000 years ago have been excavated in Utah. Of course, dogs may have hung around

Many experts believe that dogs split off from their wolf cousins about 100,000 years ago.

the fireside many years before that—as scavengers, possibly even functioning as dinner themselves and eventually as cooperative partners for hunting, guarding, and herding.

Two of those functions are to help with hunting and to guard treasured resources such as grain, poultry, and lambs. Dogs have often taken the place of additional human workers on farms. The domestication of the dog has had mutual benefits for both human and dog!

## THE DEVELOPMENT OF THE TERRIER

The British Isles are noted for the development of most of the terrier breeds. The word "terrier" itself comes from the Latin *terra*, meaning "earth." Terriers are literally "of the earth." They were bred to hunt and fight vermin such as weasels, badgers, foxes, and wildcats by going into their dens and digging them out or barking an alert to the farmer so that he would know where they were. They also worked as all-around ratters on the farm, keeping vermin from precious grain stores. As guard dogs, they would sound the alert to the presence of any predators and were perfectly willing to take chase after a wily fox.

Dogs in these work positions were selected for their toughness and gameness while facing predators. In some cases a dog might be put into a confined area with a badger or a number of rats to see who would win in a battle. The loser was often killed, but a winning male dog might be used as a stud dog and a winning female dog as a brood bitch.

## EARLY DEVELOPMENT OF THE WESTIE

The West Highland White Terrier was developed in the Argyllshire area of Scotland. This is a region known for its rocky ground, cold, wet winters, and tough vermin. Farmers needed a dog who could dig when needed to get at vermin but who was also capable of slipping between rocky crags and clambering over rocky areas to get to the vermin dens, which were often simply breaks in the rocks. Life was tough for farmers in that area, and every piece of grain was precious. Keeping the grain supplies safe, along with livestock such as poultry, was an important job for a family's terriers.

The Westie is perfectly designed for these conditions. His narrow, heart-shaped chest lets him squeeze in between tight rocks; his feet and nails are sturdy for digging; and his white coat makes him stand out against the dark ground. That rough, natural white coat is superb at shedding dirt once it dries and has kept Westies warm and fairly dry even in the rough conditions of Scotland's Argyllshire region. Some of the independence that shows up in our pet Westies of today comes from

working alone underground—
out of sight and hearing of the
farmers. The history of the breed
is often revealed in the actions and
behaviors of Westies themselves.

## THE FIRST WESTIES

The original "Highland terrier"
was most similar to today's Cairn
Terrier. A rough, sandy-colored
coat was common, but other
colors did show up on occasion.

The first possible reports of a
white terrier breed may come
from an account of dogs being
shipped to King Henry IV of
France as a gift by James VI of
Scotland in the late 1500s (who
was shortly to become king of England upon the death of Elizabeth I in 1603).
However, the exact color of the dogs is somewhat in question. Still, many Westie
fanciers like to claim that some white terriers were among the gifted dogs.

A terrier who certainly appears to be a Westie is one of two dogs in a painting
from the early 1800s by Sir Edwin Landseer called *Dignity and Impudence*. Dignity
is represented by a Bloodhound, while impudence is definitely a fit description
for the small white terrier depicted!

The original "Highland
terrier" was most
similar to today's Cairn
Terrier, pictured here.

## COLONEL EDWARD DONALD MALCOLM FROM POLTALLOCH

Certainly small white terriers were in existence for at least 100 years before
the "father of the breed," Colonel Edward Donald Malcolm of Poltalloch in
Scotland, started selectively breeding these dogs in the 1800s. Both his father and
grandfather had also bred some white or light-colored terriers. Prior to Colonel
Malcolm's breeding program, many farmers felt that white or light-colored terriers
were inferior and culled them because those colors can be associated with
genetic defects in some animals. However, that is not the case with the West
Highland White Terrier.

Colonel Malcolm became convinced that he wanted only white or very
light-colored terriers after he accidentally shot a favorite ginger-colored dog
of his while hunting. The reddish color led him to mistake his dog for a fox. His

Poltalloch terriers were widely known for their working and hunting ability, though—not just their white coats.

### DR. FLAXMAN FROM FIFE

Meanwhile, Dr. Flaxman from Fife on the eastern coast of Scotland was also breeding white terriers—his were from a Scottish Terrier bitch who tended to produce at least one or two white or light puppies in her litters. (There are wheaten-colored Scotties seen today.) These dogs had a slightly longer head and muzzle but excellent dark pigment. They were known as Pittenweem Terriers. Some of these terriers had a cream coloring to their coats.

### THE DUKE OF ARGYLL FROM ROSENEATH

A third strain of white terriers was simultaneously being developed by the Duke of Argyll from Roseneath. His dogs also had a slightly longer head than the Colonel's line, as well as slightly softer coats. Their coats were usually pure white, though.

### THE RESULT OF THE THREE TERRIER LINES

In many ways, the three lines of white terriers were similar. They all were fairly small, straight-legged, flexible enough to squeeze between rocky crags, and game

Colonel Edward Donald Malcolm of Poltalloch is considered the father of the breed.

The Westie's rough coat protects him from the harsh winter weather of snow, sleet, and freezing rain.

enough to dig and go into dens. A strong bark to alert the farmer/hunter to their location was also important. A rougher coat that would simply allow dirt to slide off with a good shake was preferred. The rough coat also protected the dog from the harsh winter weather of snow, sleet, and freezing rain. Undoubtedly there was some interbreeding of the three lines, but each line stayed true to its original type and differences.

Still, dog show judges at this time tended to favor the Poltalloch type, and it is the Colonel's type that prevailed to lead to the Westie we know today. The Colonel tried to unify the breed by bringing the breeders of various types together. He is said to be responsible for the name West Highland White Terrier in an attempt to create a better camaraderie amongst the breeders.

## EARLY SHOW DOGS AND BREED CLUBS

In 1860 in Birmingham, England, Westies made their first debut at a dog show. The West Highland White Terrier Club was later formed in Scotland in 1904, with the Duke of Argyll as president. The British club was formed right about then as well, with Colonel Malcolm as the vice president. The dogs were not officially known as West Highland White Terriers until 1907, when the breed first appeared at Crufts (England's national dog show), however. In 1908 a total of 141 Westies was registered in the British Isles.

Many of the early show dogs literally came right off the farm to the dog show. Some showed honorable badges of work such as scars or torn ears from their work catching vermin. There was a determination on the part of many breeders to distinguish these white terriers from the light-colored Scottish Terriers because interbreeding between some of the smaller terrier breeds was still occurring.

## THE SAVIOR OF THE BREED

Mrs. Cyril (May) Pacey of England is credited with being the savior of the Westie in the early 1900s. Her "Wolvey" Westies provided the foundation stock for many Westie kennels both in England and abroad. Despite the cessation of shows during the World Wars and serious problems raising and feeding dogs with rationing, Mrs. Pacey managed to keep her kennel and the Westie breed alive. At one point during the severe rationing of World War I she had to euthanize 15 of her dogs because she couldn't feed them. When World War II loomed, she sent some of her top dogs abroad to try to save them.

When looking at photos of Mrs. Wolvey and her Westies from the 1930s, you can easily recognize the Westies we see today. Breed type was set by then and has been faithfully maintained. Some of Mrs. Wolvey's Westies ended up in Canada and the United States.

## ENGLISH AND AMERICAN WESTIES

After the World Wars, the Westie surged to popularity in England. In 1950 a Westie named Shiningcliff Simon captured Best Terrier at the renowned Crufts dog show. Westies were on the rise! (More recently, the English Westie Ch. Olac Moon Pilot won Best in Show at Crufts in 1990.)

In 1908 the American Kennel Club (AKC) admitted Westies but under the Roseneath Terrier name. That was changed in 1909 to the West Highland White Terrier, and the same standard as the British one was adopted.

Up until 1917, there were still some interbreedings of Cairns and Westies, with puppies being registered by color as much as parentage. At that time, the AKC put a stop to the interbreeding. The English Kennel Club took similar action about the same time. The breeds have evolved separately since, with modern Westies being about 1 inch (2.5 cm) taller and 3 pounds (1.5 kg) heavier than the average Cairn Terrier.

## NATIONAL WESTIE CLUBS

The West Highland White Terrier Club of America (WHWTCA) was formed in 1909, while the Canadian West Highland White Terrier Club (CWHWTC) was

Local and regional clubs provide a way for Westie fanciers to get together on a more frequent and casual basis.

formed in 1952. Many lovely Westies exist in Canada as well as the United States, and breedings frequently take place across the border.

There are currently many clubs for the West Highland White Terrier in North America. Both the Canadian and American parent clubs (primary clubs representing the breed in their respective countries) are responsible for setting the blueprint or standard for the breed, but they do much more. Parent clubs also have a number of regional clubs. The regional clubs are scattered about the countries and serve to provide shows and support for Westie owners throughout the countries.

Both parent clubs provide a wealth of information about Westies, activities, care, and training on their websites. The two clubs are also active in supporting rescue and health research for Westies. If you are considering an adult Westie, you might want to check out their rescue sites first. In addition, the national and regional clubs sell Westie items to help support club projects, including rescue costs and health research.

Local and regional clubs provide a way for Westie fanciers to get together on a more frequent and casual basis. Regional clubs may also sponsor classes at a show, hold their own specialty shows, and help to put on a national specialty. Many regional clubs hold fun days for their members to try different dog sports such as earthdog or tracking. Members might offer mini-seminars on hand-stripping or give talks about nutrition and training. A club can be a fun way for you to learn more about Westies and spend time with other Westie lovers.

The Westie clubs also are the backbone for Westie rescue and health research. Clubs may hold fundraisers or ask members to do home checks for prospective foster or forever homes for Westies in need. You can do your part to help the breed you love as a member of a Westie club, whether it is a monetary donation for a good cause or offering your home as a foster home for a Westie. Be forewarned—many foster homes end up being "forever homes"!

In fact, many families start out with a rescued or rehomed Westie from a reputable breeder. The Westie clubs can provide listings of reputable breeders who have signed the code of ethics and who have puppies available. Expect to be grilled—reputable breeders are tough about who "adopts" their puppies. Getting a puppy from a reputable breeder and joining a Westie club means that you will have plenty of mentoring advice available.

## THE WEST HIGHLAND WHITE TERRIER CLUB OF AMERICA (WHWTCA)

The WHWTCA is a very active parent club. Each year there are two national specialty shows—one of them held as part of the famous Montgomery Kennel Club Terrier cluster—as well as obedience and rally trials, earthdog tests, and tracking tests. (See Chapter 9 for more information on these exciting sports.) All of these events showcase the conformation of the Westie and the working abilities that these terriers still retain.

Many families start out with a rescued or rehomed Westie from a reputable breeder.

In addition to competitions, the Westie club provides educational seminars, provides support materials for Westie owners, and supports research into health matters that involve the breed. They publish an informative magazine all about Westies called the

From the time they were recognized until today, Westies' popularity has continued to grow.

*Westie Imprint* that includes training tips, care and education, and even show results. Club members receive the magazine as a benefit, but you can subscribe to learn more about Westies before joining. Some regional clubs will also publish magazines or newsletters. The club magazines may provide listings of reputable breeders and let you know who has litters with puppies available for adoption.

Breeders, show fanciers, and pet owners are all welcome to apply for membership in the WHWTCA. You will need two sponsors who are members of the club and have known you for at least two years. If you got a puppy from a reputable breeder or a rehomed dog through a breeder or rescue, you should have no trouble getting sponsors. Attending regional club meetings is another way to get to know members. It can be a good idea to meet other Westie owners by attending local dog shows. (Always wait until the breed judging is over to approach people showing Westies, however. Prior to judging they will be busy with grooming and prepping their dogs, plus dealing with their show nerves.) All prospective members must sign a code of ethics designed to keep the breed safe and sound.

## THE CANADIAN WEST HIGHLAND WHITE TERRIER CLUB (CWHWTC)

The CWHWTC is also a very active club. This club requires you to find a sponsor (it could be your Westie's breeder) and to sign a code of ethics as well. The *Westie*

*News* is the club newsletter and is filled with tips about caring for and training your dog.

## TOP-RANKING WESTIES

Westies have done well at the big shows in the United States. In 1942 a bitch imported from Mrs. Pacey of Great Britain, Ch. Wolvey Pattern of Edgarstoune, earned Best in Show honors at the Westminster Kennel Club show in the United States. She was one of the Westies Mrs. Pacey had sent abroad to avoid the war issues in Great Britain.

In 1960 an imported Westie named Ch. Symmetra Snip became the first Westie to take top honors at the Montgomery County Kennel Club show, which is an all-terrier specialty.

In 1962 another Westie took the top spot at Westminster, this time a dog named Ch. Elfinbrook Simon. This charming fellow also won the national specialty show for Westies in 1962. Television broadcasting made him a national hero. That win helped solidify the position of Westies as top show dogs and companions. Westies have taken the Terrier Group first place three times since then, along with five Group 2s, six Group 3s, and one Group 4. Because the Terrier Group consists of all the Best of Breed Terriers at the show, this is quite an accomplishment. A Group 1 means that the Westie was the best terrier at Westminster that year, a Group 2 the second-best terrier at Westminster that year, etc. Not bad for a small white dog of the earth!

In 2006 Ch. Camcrest Bebe Queen of Trouble placed fourth in the tough Terrier Group at Eukanuba in Long Beach, California. So Westies are not strangers to the top spots at any of the big, invitation-only dog shows.

Most recently, the Westie C. Blythfell Fergus, bred and owned by Carol Hufnagel, took a Group 4 in the Terrier Group at Westminster in 2011, charming the large crowd both at Madison Square Garden and at home on national television.

## THE WESTIE'S GROWING POPULARITY

Of all AKC breeds, the West Highland White Terrier has consistently ranked in the top third or higher. In 2010 the Westie stood in 34th place. Along with Miniature Schnauzers, they are the most popular terrier. (Yorkshire Terriers are actually a Toy Group breed, and Boston Terriers belong to the Non-Sporting Group.) From the time the breed was recognized until today, the Westie's popularity has continued to grow!

# CHARACTERISTICS OF YOUR WEST HIGHLAND WHITE TERRIER

Your Westie, you will quickly learn, is a unique little character. Each Westie is a special individual shaped by his genetics, his early rearing, and his life experiences. Even so, there are some characteristics that most, if not all, Westies share.

## PHYSICAL APPEARANCE

The physical appearance of a breed includes the characteristics that mark it as a certain type of dog. There are not many dog breeds that come only in some shades of white and even fewer small dogs who are white in color. Add in the Westie's prick ears and jaunty tail and you have a distinct picture in your mind.

### BODY TYPE

The Westie's body should be sturdy in appearance. You will hear people refer to Westies as having a "heart-shaped" chest so that they could easily squeeze in between rocky crags in the past. You should have an impression of balance when you look at a Westie standing off to the side. He's a big dog in a small package who moves with a smooth and easy gait.

### SIZE

While Westies are not large dogs by any means, they are sturdy for their size. The average Westie stands about 10 to 11 inches (25.5 cm to 28 cm) tall and weighs

While Westies are not large dogs, they are sturdy for their size.

about 15 to 20 pounds (7 to 9 kg). A male Westie will generally weigh a bit more than a female. Ideally, a Westie is just a touch shorter in the back length than he is tall. He will have sturdy bones in his legs—all the better to dig with!

## COAT

Although a good Westie coat is harsh and basically wash and wear, it will require some attention. You should plan on at least weekly thorough groomings. If you choose to hand-strip your Westie, you may want to plan short daily sessions. A pet-type clip can relieve a great deal of the grooming work, but you will need to plan for trips to the groomer and the expense involved—unless, of course, you learn to clip him yourself. No matter what, you need to plan to spend some time on coat care.

## COAT COLOR

Your Westie, just as his name indicates, is white. Of course if you have ever looked at paint chips for white paint, you know that there are many, many shades of white. The softer undercoat is almost always a bright white. The harsh outercoat may be pure white or may have some wheaten (flax or tan colored) shadings to it. How the coat is cared for and the diet your Westie eats may affect the "shade" of white.

## HEAD

Photos of Westie puppies are adorable because of the great contrast between the darkly pigmented nose and the bright but dark eyes and the bright white coat. Westies tend to have nice dark pigment, so the eye rims should be black like mascara, and the nose should be all black. The lips will be black too but not the tongue. The head, if trimmed properly, will appear to be round. You may hear people refer to Westies as having a "chrysanthemum" shape to their heads. The "eyebrows" created as part of the trim add to the overall cute appearance.

## EARS

The jaunty little pointy ears that stand up proudly add to the overall expression

The Westie's tail is referred to as "carrot shaped" and is carried straight up.

of intelligence and perhaps mischief. While your Westie resembles a cute stuffed teddy bear, don't be fooled. His jaws and teeth are strong. Remember, a Westie was bred to fight with tough animals!

## NECK

Your Westie should have a nice neck, blending into his back smoothly. The neck needs to be fairly sturdy so that he can drag vermin out of dens if need be—or at least drag his toys and blankets around the house!

## FEET

The front feet of a Westie are round, with the hind feet slightly smaller. The pads are usually dark in color and thick, with the nails generally dark and thick as well. Those qualities are helpful for running across rough terrain and digging through rocky ground.

## TAIL

Even the tail of a Westie is sturdy. It is referred to as having a "carrot shape" and is carried straight up. The tail carriage fits with the Westie personality: outgoing and ready for anything and everything.

# LIVING WITH A WESTIE

In attitude, a Westie is aware of everything around him but friendly and not aggressive. He is a small dog with a big attitude. You will hear families describe their Westies as self-confident, self-possessed, and full of self-esteem. They may also use the phrases "stubborn," "obnoxious," "clever," and "devious." They may look like cuddly teddy bears, but they are extremely capable predators and not usually inclined to be lapdogs.

Roger Caras did the announcements and breed descriptions at the Westminster dog show for many years. His oft-quoted description of the Westie is: "When a West Highland White Terrier occupies the same room as you, he will constantly let you know of your good fortune." They're small in size but big in ego and attitude!

It is important to look at the background of Westies to know where they are coming from and how they relate to the world. These are curious, active dogs. As a group, terriers are often referred to as tenacious or "terrier tough." They had to be independent and persistent to succeed at their job of finding and killing vermin. Your average Westie may easily turn that focus and intensity on other tasks—like chewing through a door just in case there might be a mouse in the next room or digging up an entire flower bed just in case there is a mole somewhere in there.

## COMPANIONABILITY

Most Westies are social souls and enjoy meeting new people and new cats and dogs.

### With Cats

Many Westies form great alliances with the family cat. Perhaps this comes from working together on "rat patrol" centuries ago in Scottish barns! The best combination here is to add a puppy to a house with a dog-savvy cat. They seem to get along very well with farm animals as well—from sheep to horses.

### With Other Dogs

If you have adopted two Westies, especially adults who have lived together a fair amount of time, you need to be aware of "pack hunting" behaviors. While one Westie might not dare to challenge the family cat, two may figure that he is fair game. This goes for house bunnies and other small pets as well.

Westies may or may not get along with a lot of other dogs. A Westie who is raised around other dogs from puppyhood and who is well socialized may develop some strong dog-friend bonds. Other Westies are more aloof and less inclined to play or interact with other dogs. Individual personalities certainly come into play, as does socialization.

Very often Westies get along best with big dogs. After all, they have a big dog, macho personality. In your Westie's mind he is simply a white, slightly fuzzy Great Dane. Luckily, many big dogs will simply humor a tough little terrier sidekick. With dogs of other breeds, though, remember that your Westie pictures himself as a large and very tough dog. Although they don't often start arguments, they don't usually back down or walk away either. They are truly "terrier tough."

In the home, Westies of opposite sexes tend to make the best buddies. If both dogs are spayed or neutered, life is generally even easier and smoother. Two intact males may get along, but once maturity arrives you may find yourself refereeing daily battles for the "top dog" position. Neutered males, on the other hand, may form great and lifelong friendships. Two females, whether spayed or intact, may not always be best buddies.

## With Other Animals

A Westie should not be left unattended around any house bunnies or family pocket pets like guinea pigs. His instincts may be too strong, and you don't want a family disaster on your hands. It is probably best not to even try to combine

In the home, Westies of opposite sexes tend to make the best buddies.

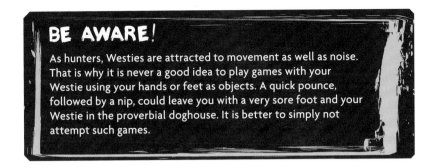

**BE AWARE!**

As hunters, Westies are attracted to movement as well as noise. That is why it is never a good idea to play games with your Westie using your hands or feet as objects. A quick pounce, followed by a nip, could leave you with a very sore foot and your Westie in the proverbial doghouse. It is better to simply not attempt such games.

a Westie with those types of pets. If, however, you end up with a combo like a Westie and a guinea pig, make sure that the guinea pig has a sturdy cage. Ideally, that cage should be in a room either locked off from your Westie by a closed door or by a sturdy baby gate.

## With Adult Humans

In general, Westies are very active and animated dogs. They love to be busy and enjoy the company of their humans. In fact, Westies are considered to be among the most people-oriented of all the terrier breeds. They want to engage in play and games with you. Be forewarned that they are adept at training you to play with them and do their bidding. Don't fall for the cute face and clever antics.

A mature Westie or even a senior rescue Westie may make the ideal companion for a senior citizen. Most younger Westies, however, may have too much energy and zip to be content quietly being a companion dog. They want action and plenty of it.

## With Small Humans

For some of those same reasons, the average Westie is not a great choice for a family with toddlers or young children. There are many reasons for this. The high-pitched squeaks of young children playing may sound like prey noises to a Westie. Remember, Westies are terriers, complete with all those hunting instincts!

In addition, small children tend to walk around with food in their hands at the ideal height for a Westie raid. The child may be traumatized, the Westie may get food he shouldn't eat, and it is even possible to have an accidental bite as the Westie tries to grab and run. If small children and a Westie need to mix, say a visit from grandchildren, it is important to supervise them at all times. A well-behaved child who throws a toy for your Westie may have a great time playing fetch. Always make sure, however, that your Westie has a private place where he can retreat if necessary. If your Westie growls or shows his teeth, he is clearly saying that he needs a break from all the commotion.

Small children and Westie puppies are an especially tricky combination. Many puppies haven't totally mastered the idea of bite inhibition. Combine that with their extremely sharp baby teeth with the curved canines and you have a disaster waiting to happen. With no malice intended you could end up with a hurt, crying toddler and a Westie triumphantly making off with a child's beloved toy.

Children over ten years of age generally have the maturity and control to be great Westie buddies.

With some coaching they could walk your Westie, care for him, and play with him. Your Westie should always have an adult human around for backup, especially if play gets too rough or he simply wears out. Any dog will resort to using his teeth if he gets pushed too far, and Westies have very strong jaws for small dogs.

*Children over ten years of age generally have the maturity and control to be great Westie buddies.*

## ENERGY LEVEL

Although adult Westies may seem to be like Energizer bunnies, Westie puppies are even more active—unless they are sound asleep. It is very important that you enforce some "downtime" right from the start with your new family member. It might work best to have a "crate nap" after a long walk or a vigorous game of fetch. Self-control is an important virtue for a Westie.

Beware of getting your Westie, adult or puppy, too riled up playing games. At times like that your Westie may go into instinctive hunt mode, and a nip may result.

## ENVIRONMENT

Westies are very adaptable small dogs who can function well in urban, suburban, and rural settings.

## Urban

Westies can do well in a city setting as long as they get plenty of walks and attention. Plan on at least two walks of good length twice a day. Young, fit Westies can easily do a mile (1.5-km) walk twice daily. Senior citizen Westies may be content with 1/10 of a mile (0.15 km). Combine that with some daily training and perhaps some games of fetch down the hallway. Luckily Westies are small enough that the noise shouldn't be too overwhelming for a downstairs neighbor. However, you will have to work to control your Westie's urge to bark. (See Chapter 8.) A terrier alarm bark is quite sharp and piercing.

## Suburban

In the suburbs, a Westie may appoint himself as the "neighborhood watchdog." From a vantage point in a window or outside in the yard, he will watch for errant squirrels and even any teenagers with a bent for vandalism. Beware of nuisance barking.

## Rural

If your Westie is lucky enough to live in the country, he will be a happy dog. He can accompany you while you work in the garden and keep all rabbits away. Westies do seem to enjoy the company of horses and vice versa, so he will happily hang out at the stable with you. Just be careful that he doesn't get under a horse or where he might get kicked.

One danger of country living for your Westie is the use of poisonous baits for rodent control. Although he may not be attracted to the bait itself, he might be

## Dog Tale

Lorri Moffa relates a story about her Westie Hopscotch. "I had a cat when I acquired my first Westie, Hopscotch. She loved food and found an ingenious way to get at it. The cat was free-fed, so his food was moved to the top of the portable dishwasher. Hopscotch figured out that when she heard the portable dishwasher in use it was in a position that she could get to. She discovered that she could jump to the countertop from a kitchen chair and then onto the top of the dishwasher. She would extend herself to get to the dishwasher but did not feel safe enough to jump down. When I arrived to empty the dishwasher, there was Hopscotch, resting after finishing off the cat food."

A nice swim is a good form of exercise for the Westie.

thrilled that he can easily catch a weakened rat. That rat may have enough poison still in its system to make your Westie very ill. So even way out in the country, it is best if your Westie acts as your companion and is not off on his own.

## EXERCISE REQUIREMENTS

Left to their own devices, Westies can become nuisance barkers, diggers, and chewers. Exercise, both physical and mental (as well as training), is important for a Westie's good health.

### Physical Exercise

Westies will not need the same exercise as a field-bred Labrador Retriever, but they are energetic dogs. A long walk once or preferably twice a day is important. You might switch that out with a swim at the lake or a vigorous training class. Playing games like fetch with your Westie will help bond him to you as well as give him some great exercise.

Many terriers are described as high energy, and Westies are no exception. Right from the start you need to recognize when your Westie is getting overstimulated and needs to take a break. Having him crate trained is invaluable for giving everyone some needed downtime. (See Chapter 7.) You may even find that your Westie seeks out his crate on his own when there is a lot of human activity in the house.

Plan your walks to avoid hot paved areas in warm weather and places with lots of ice melters in the winter. You may have to clean his feet and underside off if you walk on sidewalks.

Most dog parks allow Westies, and a well-behaved Westie can charm most people you meet. Dog parks should be used with caution. If the park is well organized with regular cleanup and health screenings for member dogs, it can be a fun place for your Westie to romp and run. Many dog parks have separate areas for large dogs and small dogs. However, if your Westie doesn't play well with others, a dog park may not be the best place for him.

If you have a yard of your own, you may want to build a dog digging pit. This is a blocked-off area with sand or gravel where you can hide toys or bones and your Westie can dig to his heart's content. Most dogs quickly learn that this is the only area in which they are allowed to dig.

Do remember that digging is bound to happen if a Westie is left outside in the yard by himself for very long. Make sure that your fences are Westie-proofed when he is loose in the yard. That may even mean needing to place some chicken wire dug into the ground around the perimeter or a cement shelf so that he can't dig his way to freedom. Also, a Westie, thanks to that heart-shaped chest, can squeeze through amazingly small openings. Check that your gates fit snugly. A tight fence will also help to keep stray wildlife out of your yard so that you aren't dealing with gifts of dead rabbits or squirrels daily.

*Having your Westie perform tricks is a great way to get rid of some of that excess energy.*

Even if you have a squirrel-infested yard, don't count on your Westie to exercise himself when left outdoors. He may run around a bit, but he may simply find a sunny spot and nap. Squirrels and other wildlife may quickly learn to avoid the yard when your Westie is out, depriving him of a chance to chase.

## Mental Exercise

Mental exercise is important too,

no matter whether you have a "city Westie" or a "country Westie." Often mental exercise can wear your Westie out just as well if not better than physical exercise. You can purchase mental exercise games for your Westie that generally involve his working out a physical puzzle to get a food treat. You can also simply teach him tricks, make him work for his food by using a hard rubber toy as a food dispenser, or train him to find toys or treats hidden around the house. Keep in mind that treats should be deducted from his daily rations or you will end up with a very round Westie. Obedience training, rally training, and agility can all wear your Westie out both physically and mentally as well. (See Chapter 9.)

## PREY DRIVE

Westies have ingrained drives to hunt prey and to dig. If they spot a squirrel running, they are going to take off after it. This doesn't mean that they can't be trained to control their prey drive, but you have to recognize that it is there and learn to handle your Westie's instincts. When a Westie is in the throes of full-blown hunting mode, he truly may not register that you are calling his name even when you are merely 5 feet (1.5 m) away.

Even an extremely well-trained Westie may lose the battle with his instincts once in a while when a squirrel dashes by. You need to keep that in mind and always have him on lead in any area that could conceivably be unsafe. On the other hand, if you have a safely fenced backyard, you may have the only bird feeders in the neighborhood not raided by squirrels because of your "Westie patrols."

Westies have ingrained drives to hunt prey and to dig.

## TRAINABILITY

Training a Westie can be a challenge. There is no question about the breed's intelligence. Just watch a Westie figure out how to get what he wants—and he won't quit until he does figure out how to get the toy out from under the couch, even if it requires chewing through a cushion! Remember that independent streak as

well and work very hard on training him to come when called. Your Westie should not be left outside alone as he will undoubtedly get into mischief. Plus you got him as a companion, so he is best off by your side.

The best training techniques for a Westie combine positive methods with firmness, consistency, and fairness. You need to have everyone who will be involved with your Westie on the same page as to commands used, how to get him to obey, and what rewards to employ. For most terrier breeds the "nothing in life is free" ideal works quite well, and Westies are no exception. For example, a Westie who learns that he has to sit politely before he gets his bedtime biscuit will learn not to jump up and grab food from someone's hand.

The best training techniques for a Westie combine positive methods with firmness, consistency, and fairness.

It is important to remember that Westies are both loyal and independent. They will happily do your bidding if they respect you or if they feel that it is worth their while. Westies do best with a firm but fair hand. Positive training techniques work very well, but be prepared to take a stand if your Westie challenges you. This is not a breed for the faint of heart or for someone who prefers to simply compromise. For your Westie, today it is the right-hand cushion on the couch; tomorrow the whole couch!

# CHAPTER 3

# SUPPLIES FOR YOUR WEST HIGHLAND WHITE TERRIER

Adding a Westie to your family means that you will need to do some fun dog supply shopping. Whether your Westie will be a new adult rescue, a rehome, or a puppy, there are certain items that will make life easier and more fun for both of you. Some of them are important and virtually essential, while others are purely for fun.

## BABY GATE

Baby gates or doorway gates aren't essential, but they can certainly make your life easier. A gate can block off an area to give your family cat some peace and quiet from an energetic Westie puppy. You can block off stairways so that you don't have to worry about a puppy falling down the stairs. Or you can block off your formal dining room with the valuable imported rug to prevent puppy accidents. By blocking off certain areas you may actually be able to give your Westie more freedom in the house.

## BED

Most Westies enjoy a bit of the luxury life even though they truly are "terrier tough." That means a soft, comfortable bed is greatly preferred to the hard floor! While your Westie is still a pup, do not invest in an expensive bed. His urge to chew as he teethes and the chance of an accident both make it likely that the bed

Westies greatly enjoy a soft, comfortable bed.

Older Westies or Westies with a heart problem or a weak trachea may benefit from using a harness instead of a collar.

will get destroyed. Instead, stick to old, comfortable blankets, comforters that are garage sale finds, or make an inexpensive pad yourself.

Most Westies appreciate some padding in their crates, so be sure that the bedding is nontoxic for your pup. Older Westies can have nice pillows, expensive cushions, etc. It is a good idea to have two or three beds or blankets to keep around the house in different locations where you often spend time. That way your Westie can curl up in comfort near you.

Watch out for materials that may give your Westie "static shocks" in the winter, like flannels and many synthetics like polyester. It is nice to have a couple of washable beds—some warm ones for winter and cooler fabric for the hot months. Eventually your Westie may earn the privilege of sleeping on your bed with you, but not all Westies work out well as bedtime companions, so make sure that yours has a comfortable place of his own to sack out.

## COLLAR

A good collar (and leash—discussed later) will help keep your Westie safe. Most Westies are comfortable with a rolled leather or nylon collar. Collars can have regular buckles or snap/quick-release buckles. The collar should not rub on the dog's neck or slip over his head too easily. If you start off with a Westie puppy, remember to check the collar size frequently. His neck will grow, and you don't want a tight collar to make him uncomfortable.

Tags can be attached to the rings on the collar. For Westies, it is nice to get a tag pouch that fits over the collar. This keeps all the tags together so that it is quieter, slows down wear and tear on the writing on the tags, and keeps the tags from leaving a metal stain on that pristine white coat. You can also have your phone number embroidered into the collar or have a plate riveted to the collar with identification info.

Older Westies or Westies with a heart problem or a weak trachea may benefit from using a harness instead of a collar. Do what works best for your individual dog.

## CRATE

Every Westie will do better in his new home if he has a safe place to go when he is tired, a safe place to rest while you are away from home, and a safe way to travel with you. The answer to those needs is a crate—and as a bonus, crates are useful for help in housetraining too! (See Chapter 7.)

There are many different types of crates from which to choose. For a new family member it is best to have a sturdy crate that can stand up to an occasional temper tantrum. Once your Westie has adjusted to your family and learns that his crate is a good and safe place to be, you may choose to switch to a canvas crate. It is a good idea to have a couple of crates: one for your bedroom for your Westie to sleep in at night, one for the car, and one to move into different rooms so that your Westie can be with you. Once he is "house-proofed," you won't need the third crate, but while you are establishing house manners it is nice to have.

### CANVAS

Canvas crates are popular because they are light and easy to carry. These crates are made of canvas with wire mesh for ventilation. Once you can feel comfortable

Plastic crates are good for the car because they will keep your Westie safe.

that your Westie won't try to chew or dig his way out of a crate, this type may be a good option for you. These portable enclosures are excellent for using in a hotel room while traveling or if you are visiting relatives. However, they are not sturdy enough to provide very much safety in a car.

## PLASTIC

Plastic crates are also quite sturdy and work well for puppies and newbie adults. Ventilation may not be as good as in a wire crate, but you do have more protection from the elements. The bottoms often include a wire rack that your Westie may not feel comfortable on, so you will need a crate pad or cushion. Some plastic kennels are approved for air travel. They are nice crates for the car because they will keep your Westie safe. There is also less visual stimulation in a plastic crate.

## WIRE

Wire crates stand up well to a teething puppy or unhappy adult. They provide plenty of ventilation, so they are good for warm weather. The bottom generally has a metal or sturdy plastic tray that can be removed for cleaning. Most Westies like to have a soft cushion or some comfortable blankets to lie on in their crates, so you may have to provide that extra bit of comfort. These crates work well for travel in your car, keeping your Westie safe and comfortable. A disadvantage is that a busybody Westie who likes to bark will be able to see everything unless you provide a cover for the crate. Wire crates can be heavy and awkward, but many fold up into "suitcases" that are easy to carry.

## EX-PEN

An ex-pen is a series of panels, usually wire, that can form a mini-corral. These are useful for confining your Westie safely but give him more freedom than a crate. An ex-pen set up in a corner may allow him to attend your dinner party without begging or annoying non-doggy friends. It can also go on trips to the park so that your Westie is safely confined while you picnic.

## FOOD AND WATER BOWLS

Food and water bowls should be easy to clean and wide enough that your Westie can easily put his muzzle in without cramping his whiskers. Ceramic or stainless steel bowls are preferable to plastic or rubber. Plastic and rubber have been associated with pigment loss on the nose and allergic reactions in some dogs. Why take the chance? There are many cute ceramic dishes—even some with

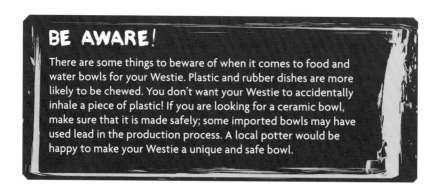

## BE AWARE!

There are some things to beware of when it comes to food and water bowls for your Westie. Plastic and rubber dishes are more likely to be chewed. You don't want your Westie to accidentally inhale a piece of plastic! If you are looking for a ceramic bowl, make sure that it is made safely; some imported bowls may have used lead in the production process. A local potter would be happy to make your Westie a unique and safe bowl.

Westie themes! For a sturdy, unbreakable option, stainless steel may be your best choice. Whatever you decide, plan to wash the dishes daily.

## GROOMING SUPPLIES

What you will need to keep your Westie looking up to snuff will depend partly on whether you plan to clip him, have him groomed by a groomer, or "strip" his coat. (See Chapter 5 for grooming details.) There are some basics that every Westie will need, however.

### BRUSHES AND COMBS

A slicker brush is excellent for brushing the hair on the legs and tail plus the skirts if your Westie has any long hair. A stripping "knife" can be helpful if you want to keep your Westie in a natural coat without any clipping. Your breeder can guide you there. A pin brush and a terrier palm pad are both nice grooming tools to own even if your Westie makes regular trips to the groomer. A good-quality comb is important for detangling areas that might mat, such as the armpits.

### GROOMING TABLE

Some families invest in a grooming table to help save their backs when cleaning up their Westie. You can also make one inexpensively by purchasing a small collapsible table and gluing a small rug or bath mat on the top to keep your Westie from slipping. Never leave him alone on a grooming table—he could badly injure himself jumping off.

### NAIL CLIPPERS

A nail clipper or Dremel-type rotary tool to wear down toenails is important. Nail clippers can be guillotine or scissor type. Without regular trims, your Westie could get broken or cracked nails, which are very painful. Also, long nails can make your Westie's paws splay out and put abnormal pressure on his joints. Left untrimmed, nails can even grow around into the pads, especially if your Westie has his dewclaws left on.

## SCISSORS

Some scissors can be important for "touch-up" areas on your Westie. Thinning shears can help keep him looking good between grooming appointments. Straight scissors can be used to trim long hair on his legs or sides. And a pair of small blunt-ended scissors is excellent for trimming around his feet and between his pads.

Thinning scissors can help keep your Westie looking great between grooming appointments.

## TOWELS

A couple of designated "dog towels" are important for drying your Westie off when he comes in from the rain, after a bath, or after a romp in the snow.

## IDENTIFICATION

It is important that your Westie has some form of identification. With their skill at digging and squeezing through tight places, along with their urge to explore, Westies can easily sneak out of a yard and escape. Identification does two things: 1.) It helps your Westie find his way home if he's found; and 2.) It could serve to prove that your Westie truly is a member of your family.

Most municipalities have laws requiring that stray dogs who are picked up wearing a collar and tags along with a tattoo or with a microchip must be held longer in the shelter than a stray with no identification. It is definitely worth your while to have identification for your Westie! You could gain as many as three to five days of safety for him while you search for him.

## TAGS

All Westies should be licensed. States or communities have license tags that allow for identification of your dog and also provide phone numbers to call to help return him. Rabies tags also have individual numbers for each dog, along with a phone number to your Westie's veterinary clinic.

Many pet supply stores have machines to make unique identification tags for your Westie right in the store. You can put on his name, your phone number,

The best leash for your Westie is one that is comfortable for you.

or whatever information you choose. Some groups recommend putting only a phone number on so that a thief won't know your Westie's name or your address.

## MICROCHIPS

Some form of permanent identification is also a good idea for your Westie, like a microchip. A microchip is a tiny silicone chip implanted under your dog's skin that has a unique number for your dog. When read with a scanner, this number appears on the screen. Depending on the format of the number, it is noted as coming from a certain microchip registry. Most animal shelters and many veterinary clinics have scanners, including universal models, that can read chips from all of the manufacturers.

Your Westie may have arrived with a microchip put in by his breeder. If not, you can get him microchipped at your veterinary clinic or look for clinics offered by dog clubs in your area. It may hurt a tiny bit when it is injected under the skin, but many dogs don't even whimper.

Whoever has found your Westie can then call the registry and make contact with you. Note that the microchip only works to help return your Westie if you have sent in the paperwork registering him with that chip. Otherwise there is no way to know who owns the dog with that specific chip number.

## TATTOOS

If you have your dog tattooed (although tattoos have fallen somewhat out of favor since microchipping is so easy to do and to read), this is sometimes done at the veterinary hospital while your Westie is being spayed or neutered. Just like a microchip, the tattoo should be registered. Most microchip companies will accept tattoos for their registries. The registries also give you a collar tag for your Westie stating that he has permanent identification. The collar tag alone may deter a thief.

## LEASH

The best leash is one that is comfortable for you! You should also look for a leash size that fits your Westie—he doesn't need a 1-inch (2.5-cm) wide thick leather leash with a huge brass snap. Nylon or soft leather works well, while chain with a plastic handle can be very uncomfortable. A 6-foot (2-m) lead is generally plenty long enough for walks.

The snap should be appropriate for your Westie. A huge snap is an unnecessary weight for his neck, while a tiny snap may break if he lunges after a squirrel. Many pet stores will let your Westie come in so that you can custom fit him.

You may want to try a retractable leash for when your Westie goes on long hikes. These should be used with care. The cord can cut both of you if you get tangled. You also don't want him disappearing around a corner where you can't see him. He could easily get into trouble. Dogs have also been injured by retractable leashes when a person accidentally drops the handle and it flies at speed to the dog and hits him. Still, if used with some care, a retractable lead can give your Westie more room to explore and a bit more exercise on your daily walks. Retractable leads do come in different sizes based on dog weight, so pick the right size for your Westie.

## TOYS

Toys are very important both to and for your Westie. These are active, bright, energetic little dogs who love being busy. If you don't provide suitable toys, they will come up with some on their own—possibly including expensive shoes, furniture, etc.

## PUPPY POINTER

There are many very sturdy hard rubber toys that can be filled with small dog treats or foods like doggy liver paste. If you need to get some work done, set your Westie puppy up near you, possibly in an ex-pen or crate, along with a treat-filled toy. This will keep him busy, quiet, and happy!

Truly, your Westie's favorite toy is you. Playing games with you, going for walks with you, and training with you are the best ways to keep your dog occupied and happy.

## FUZZY TOYS

Westies love fuzzy toys with squeakers inside, but they should not be left alone with them. With their terrier instincts and strong jaws, most Westies quickly "disembowel" their toys and may swallow stuffing or the squeaker itself. They will also cheerfully spread toy stuffing throughout the house. These are fun toys for you to play with together, and they are excellent for a game of fetch indoors.

## HARD RUBBER TOYS

Some of the best toys are hard rubber toys. Many of these toys have places where you can hide treats inside to keep your darling occupied even longer if you need to do some work.

When your Westie puppy is teething, he might enjoy having his toys put in the refrigerator or freezer for a short time. Chewing or "gumming" on the cold rubber can be soothing to those sore gums.

Westies love to play with toys but should be closely supervised.

## Dog Tale

Pam Whittle's Westie Angus loved the rubber ball that she used for a game as a teacher. Each night when she came home from work, he would pull the ball out of her bag and parade around with it. This was not a safe toy to leave with him, but he obviously enjoyed all the scents on the ball. One night Pam said he pulled her wallet out too and extracted a $20 bill! She figured he was planning to go off and buy his own supply of balls.

### TENNIS BALLS

Tennis balls are fun for a game of fetch, but don't leave them alone with your Westie. Those strong jaws can easily break the balls up, and rubber pieces or the covering could be swallowed. Dogs who chew on tennis balls too often can also wear their teeth down from the abrasive coating.

### TUG TOYS

A sturdy tug toy or two is a lot of fun as well. Just make sure that your Westie learns to "give" when you tell him to. Tugs can be made of hard rubber, braided fleece, or tightly woven string. Again, these toys should not be left alone with your Westie.

### TOYS TO AVOID

Avoid toys that resemble items you don't want your Westie to chew or bite. That means no old shoes, tied-up socks, or clothing items. Your Westie, especially while in puppyhood, won't be able to tell the difference between your valuable shoes and his play shoe. On the other hand, thick cardboard tubes can provide hours of fun as long as you don't mind picking up mushy cardboard when the game ends.

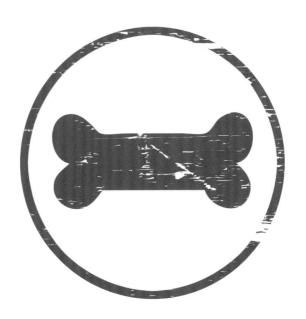

# FEEDING YOUR WEST HIGHLAND WHITE TERRIER

**M**ost Westies are not gourmets and in fact will not only eat anything and everything you put in front of them but will also actively search out things to taste and try. Still, the adage "You are what you eat" applies to our canine companions, and you want to be sure that your Westie gets all the nutrients he needs.

Your Westie's ideal dinner might be fresh rabbit with a mouse snack on the side. But your job is to provide him with the nutritional equivalent of that natural diet in a safe and healthy way—avoiding parasites, balancing nutrients, and giving him adequate nutrition for his life stage and lifestyle. A growing puppy, a senior Westie, and a Westie in his prime who is running agility courses and flying through tunnels in earthdog competitions all have different nutritional requirements. Keep in mind that each Westie is an individual and may do better on a different diet than previous Westies you owned. Even in one household you may find that your Westies do better on individualized diets.

## NUTRITIONAL BASICS

To function at his best, your Westie needs a mix of nutrients in his diet, including carbohydrates, fats, minerals, proteins, vitamins, and water.

### CARBOHYDRATES

While "carbohydrates" may seem like a dirty word in today's nutritional scene, they do have their uses. Wild canids eat berries and fruits, pick at ripe grains, and eat the fermented grains in the intestines of their prey. Your Westie can use some carbohydrates for energy, and he may need extra fiber for certain health problems. Carbohydrates may also provide some vitamins and minerals he requires. Still, carbohydrates should make up only a small portion of his diet. Carbohydrates are generally provided as grains in dog foods. Your Westie may supplement that himself by plucking fresh blackberries, blueberries, and raspberries or searching out wild strawberries.

### FATS

Fats are important for your dog for energy and a healthy coat and skin. Fats provide more than double the energy of carbohydrates. You need to be careful that your Westie doesn't get too much fat, or he will become quite round! The fat portion of his diet will provide

Carbohydrates are generally provided as grains in dog foods.

Fats are important for your dog for energy and a healthy coat and skin.

essential fatty acids, helping his immune system and keeping his skin and coat healthy. Fats can be provided as animal fat, fish oils, or plant oils. Animal fat and fish oils are generally best. The fats in your Westie's diet are the reason for most of the preservatives. You should look for a diet preserved with vitamins E and C. Never feed your Westie any food that smells rancid!

## MINERALS

Minerals are essential for healthy bones, many enzymes, and the normal functioning of many tissues—including heart muscle. Calcium and phosphorus are the two minerals most families recognize right away, and these need to be provided in the correct balance for your Westie. That ratio will change as he develops from a rapidly growing puppy to an adult dog. Some minerals will be present in other food ingredients, but others may be added separately to make sure that his diet has adequate amounts.

## PROTEINS

Protein is important for your dog as the basic requirement for muscle, many enzymes, the immune system, growth, and strength. Wild canids get their protein from the meat of the animals they kill or scavenge. But your pet Westie depends on you to round up his protein!

The actual amount of protein your individual Westie needs depends on a number of factors. Puppies need extra for growth, and very active dogs need more. Sedate senior Westies can get by with less protein.

The quality of the protein is just as important, or more so, than the amount. Proteins are made of small units called amino acids. Dogs must get ten essential amino acids in their diet for good health. These amino acids are arginine, methionine, histidine, phenylalanine, isoleucine, threonine, leucine, tryptophan, lysine, and valine. A top-quality protein will contain most, if not all, of these amino acids. Proteins with plenty of essential amino acids are said to have a high "biological value." An example of a top-quality biological value protein is an egg. After all, an egg has everything included that is necessary to grow a chicken!

## VITAMINS

Vitamins frequently get partnered with minerals because they often work hand in hand to keep your Westie healthy. Calcium needs vitamin D to be absorbed properly, for example. The water-soluble vitamins (vitamins that are not stored in the body) are vitamin C and the many B vitamins. Fat-soluble vitamins (vitamins that are stored in body fat) are A, D, E, and K. The exact amounts of vitamins in your Westie's diet are important. While extra water-soluble vitamins may simply be urinated away, fat-soluble vitamins can build up in tissues over time and cause toxicity. Your Westie needs just the right amount of vitamins—not too many and not too few.

## WATER

Water is a nutrient we tend to forget about, but it is extremely important. Your Westie could survive for days without eating, but he needs to drink frequently.

Water should be available 24/7, with the exception of close to bedtime for puppies who are still going through housetraining. Water should be fresh and offered in clean bowls. If your family needs to drink bottled water or must boil it because of a water problem, you should follow the same guidelines for your Westie. To prevent stomach upset, it is a good idea to bring extra water from home

Your Westie needs to drink water frequently.

along for your Westie when you travel. Don't let him drink from creeks and streams that might contain parasites.

## DOG FOOD LABELS

Your first duty as head cook and doggy dish washer is to learn to read labels. The label will give you the ingredients a food contains, along with a guaranteed analysis. The guaranteed analysis tells you how much of a certain type of nutrient, such as protein or fat, is contained in a food. This is the minimum amount that the company promises is present in every serving.

### COMPARING FOODS

One of the trickiest parts of figuring out nutrients is that you must be able to compare dry foods against canned foods. Dry foods have a moisture content of about 10 percent, while canned foods may have 80 percent moisture. Using that example, the dry food may claim to have 25 percent protein. Since you know that the food is 90 percent dry matter, you divide the 25 percent by 90 percent. Then multiply by 100. This will tell you that you have 27— actually almost 28—percent protein. Your canned food sample has 80 percent moisture and says 7 percent protein. At first glance, the dry food appears much higher in protein. But you need to correct for the amount of moisture. You have 20 percent dry matter, so you divide that into the 7 percent protein and multiply by 100. Whoa! Now you see that there is a whopping 35 percent protein!

### GUARANTEED ANALYSIS

Federal regulations require that a pet food must provide you with the minimum guaranteed analysis for crude protein and crude fat. "Crude" is not a descriptive statement about the fat or protein but simply refers to the process used to determine how much is present. The maximum amount of crude fiber and moisture present must also be shown on the guaranteed analysis. Some foods will include certain vitamins or minerals.

Still, guaranteed analysis takes you only so far in evaluating a food. It doesn't tell you anything about the kind or quality of protein, for instance.

## INGREDIENT LIST

The ingredient list is next on your list of importance while checking pet food labels. Ingredients are listed by their weight. This is where you need to be a thorough sleuth. You know that you want plenty of top-quality protein in your Westie's diet, and meat is the best source. So you are thrilled that chicken is listed as number one. Beware, however, that corn may show up three or four times on the ingredient list—like cornmeal, corn gluten, and whole corn. When those three forms of corn are added together, they may add up to more than the chicken that was listed first.

Toward the end of the ingredient list will be a long list of various vitamins and preservatives added to make the diet complete. Don't be overwhelmed by words like "thiamine monocitrate"—that is a source of vitamin B1.

## PRODUCT NAMES

It is also important to realize that pet food manufacturers know that they need to appeal to the humans who are buying the food for their Westies, not the

To remain healthy, a Westie must eat a nutritionally sound diet.

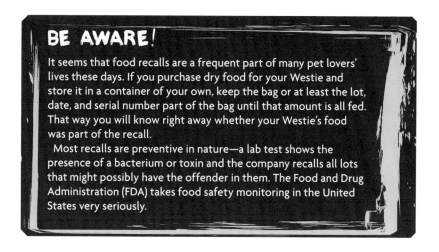

**BE AWARE!**

It seems that food recalls are a frequent part of many pet lovers' lives these days. If you purchase dry food for your Westie and store it in a container of your own, keep the bag or at least the lot, date, and serial number part of the bag until that amount is all fed. That way you will know right away whether your Westie's food was part of the recall.

Most recalls are preventive in nature—a lab test shows the presence of a bacterium or toxin and the company recalls all lots that might possibly have the offender in them. The Food and Drug Administration (FDA) takes food safety monitoring in the United States very seriously.

Westies themselves. So foods will have amazing photos on their labels of food in cut crystal serving dishes and names that make you start to salivate, such as "Beef Tenderloin in Gravy Dinner."

Product names are guided by four American Association of Feed Control Officials (AAFCO) rules.

### Rule #1

First is the 95 percent rule. The 95 percent rule is for foods with primarily meat or fish. So a canned food with 95 percent chicken can be simply called "Chicken for Dogs."

### Rule #2

Second is the 25 percent, or commonly called "dinner," rule. Under this guideline, the food must contain between 25 and 95 percent of the ingredient named. While the word "dinner" is the most common choice, it may also be called "entrée" or "platter," etc. This time your Westie is eating "Chicken Dinner" that has at least 25 percent chicken as an ingredient.

### Rule #3

The 3 percent rule means that an ingredient is present and may add something extra to the food, such as cheese for cheese flavor or tuna. It could also refer to a primary protein. So if your Westie is eating "Dog Supper With Chicken," you know that 3 percent of the food is chicken as indicated by the use of the word "with."

### Rule #4

The fourth rule is the "flavor" rule. In this case, the food must have a detectable amount of something to suggest that ingredient might be in the food. For "Dog Food With Chicken Flavor," this might mean that chicken broth is used but no actual chicken meat is present. By now, the fresh roadkill rabbit may be starting to look enticing!

## FEEDING TRIALS

An important feature of labels is whether or not the food has been tested through feeding trials. Feeding trials demonstrate that dogs actually thrive and do well on a given food. Depending on the desired label for a food, it may be tested on growing puppies, senior dogs, or active dogs in the prime of life. Always look for foods that have AAFCO feeding trials noted on the label.

# COMMERCIAL FOODS

Commercial dog foods tend to come in three varieties: canned, dry, and semi-moist. Freeze-dried foods are now becoming more popular, as are frozen raw diets. A new Westie may have a certain food that he is used to. Most breeders and rescue groups will send you home with a sample of what your Westie has been eating. If you need to change foods for some reason, do so gradually over a week or two.

For all three of the main commercial food varieties, there are foods with a wide range of quality. Store-brand foods are often lowest on the nutritional list, with premium and super-premium products near the top. Premium foods may be available only through pet stores and pet supply outlets. Some need to be ordered directly from producers.

A major advantage to commercial foods if your Westie does well on them is that they are generally always available. If you travel you can count on finding the major brands along the way. These foods have a great deal of research behind them and tend to be regulated.

There are also commercial diets designed for health problems. These are usually prescription diets, and your veterinarian may recommend one of them if your Westie has certain health problems. There are now multiple brands of these medical diets and often both canned and dry versions. Your Westie will usually find at least one version that he likes.

## CANNED FOODS

Canned foods have the most moisture, so a Westie eating canned food may not

drink as much as other Westies. Canned foods tend to be very appetizing and can be excellent for picky eaters and sick dogs whose appetites need stimulating. They do tend to be more expensive. This is where the smaller size of a Westie is a benefit!

## DRY FOODS

Dry foods are very popular because they are less expensive in general. They can be left out without big worries over spoilage if you have a Westie who likes to dawdle over his meals or prefers to pick at his food for a while. Dry foods may help a bit with tartar and plaque on your dog's teeth as well.

## SEMI-MOIST FOODS

Semi-moist foods may appeal to your dog, but they are generally not recommended. The processing for the semi-moist state often means that more sugars and preservatives are included, which aren't ideal for most dogs.

## NONCOMMERCIAL FOODS

Some Westie owners feel that their dogs do best on homemade meals. Those meals may be served raw or cooked. If you decide to prepare your Westie's food at home, you can easily make up a large amount and put it in small containers in the freezer. With a Westie you won't need a "dog-dedicated" freezer as you would with a Newfoundland!

Westies with certain health problems may benefit from home-prepared meals that limit ingredients and preservatives. You can also try different proteins to see which work best for your Westie. Your veterinarian can provide you with special recipes if your Westie needs a medical diet and is not willing to eat commercial foods.

If your Westie has any food allergies, you can try different commercial diets, but you may find that home-prepared meals are the best for him. Generally it is fairly easy to avoid the proteins that cause problems when you make your own meals. Beef and dairy products are often high on the allergen list. Remember that you need to avoid the allergenic foods in treats as well as in your Westie's regular meals.

Your dog's treats should come out of his daily food ration.

## RAW FOODS

Raw foods include everything from prepared commercial diets that can be purchased in frozen blocks to fresh chicken wings purchased at your grocery store. Most raw food diets rely heavily on meat with a few additives to balance the diet. Some Westie fanciers feel that there are fewer problems with allergies with a raw diet as a result of fewer ingredients and often single-protein sources. They also feel that it is a more "natural" diet for their dogs.

Raw diets need to be balanced. Simply throwing chicken wings at your Westie twice a day is not an adequate diet. You must also be careful to practice excellent food preparation hygiene and avoid bacterial contamination that might cause illnesses, such as diarrhea.

If you choose to try raw foods, consult a nutritionist to be sure that you make your dog's meals balanced and complete. You don't want to miss out on any essential vitamins or minerals, for example. Most veterinary colleges now have nutritionists on staff who can provide you with assistance.

When using raw foods you need to take extra precautions on hygiene and practice safe food handling. If you or anyone in your household has any immune problems, or if you have an infant in the family, it is best to avoid raw foods. Bacterial contamination, such as by *E. coli* or *Salmonella*, on food prep surfaces can be very serious in infants, elderly people, and anyone with immune problems.

### HOME-COOKED FOODS

Some families enjoy cooking for their Westies. There are many neat recipes available, some of which will work for the whole family—human and dog! If you want to develop your own recipes, have them evaluated by a vet or nutritionist to be sure that they are nutritionally complete for your Westie. A complete and balanced diet with the correct ratios of vitamins and minerals is especially important for growing puppies.

## FEEDING TIMES

Most dogs tend to thrive on a set schedule for meals. You may find that your Westie even lets you know when it is getting close to dinnertime!

### FREE-FEEDING

Free-feeding, or leaving food down all the time, has a number of disadvantages. You may not be able to tell whether your dog is actually eating on any given day. The food could go bad. And if you have more than one Westie, one dog may be eating all the food and the other dog going without. Food fights could break out between multiple dogs with food as the resource they both want. Also, many dogs will tend to overeat with food available in front of them all the time.

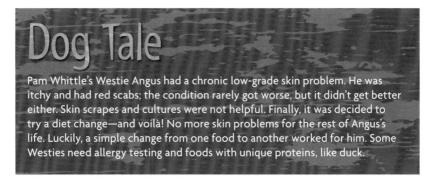

**Dog Tale**

Pam Whittle's Westie Angus had a chronic low-grade skin problem. He was itchy and had red scabs; the condition rarely got worse, but it didn't get better either. Skin scrapes and cultures were not helpful. Finally, it was decided to try a diet change—and voilà! No more skin problems for the rest of Angus's life. Luckily, a simple change from one food to another worked for him. Some Westies need allergy testing and foods with unique proteins, like duck.

## SCHEDULED FEEDING

Adult dogs can get by with just one meal a day, but for both health and mental reasons, it can be better to feed twice a day. Splitting meals means that your Westie won't be so ravenous that he gulps his food down. He will also be slightly less likely to eat any prey he catches—don't count on that, though.

A second meal also means another chance for you to interact with your Westie. Some days you might be so busy that feeding time is the only time you are together. And a dog who is dieting does much better with two meals than one. In addition, the second meal gives you another chance to be sure that your Westie is feeling fine and eating normally. That could give you a 12-hour jump on an illness.

Dogs with certain illnesses do better having their meals spread out. A diabetic Westie needs a very set mealtime regimen, but older dogs with liver or kidney problems also tend to do better with split meals.

Puppies definitely need more than one meal per day. A Westie puppy is quite small but has a huge energy requirement. Multiple meals are important for his growth and health. Many breeders have puppies on a schedule of three or four meals a day. Try to follow that schedule until your pup is about four months old. At that point, three meals a day should be adequate and you can usually cut back to twice a day at about six months of age.

## OBESITY

Obesity is a serious problem with our dogs. Even active dogs like Westies may become overweight if they are free-feeding and not getting enough exercise. A recent national study estimates that 45 percent of all dogs are either obese or overweight. Certainly some Westies must be in that study!

The weight range for Westies varies quite a bit—from 15 to 20 pounds (7 to 9 kg). Even 1 or 2 extra pounds (.5 or 1 kg) is a significant overload for these small terriers. Obesity

Even active dogs like Westies may become overweight if they are free-feeding and not getting enough exercise.

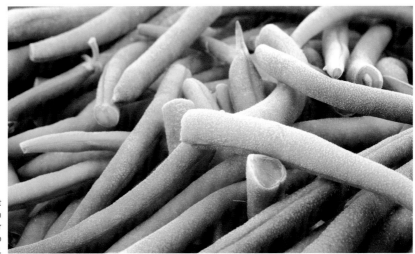

Check with your vet about adding frozen green beans to your obese Westie's diet to help him feel fuller.

puts strains on joints and multiple organs and increases the risk of heart disease and diabetes—just as in people. If your Westie is getting round and no longer has a "waist" when viewed from above, talk to your veterinarian about a diet and exercise plan. Often small adjustments may be all that you need.

There are special weight loss diets, including prescription diets, that are quite strict. You should discuss these diets with your veterinarian if your Westie is truly obese. Many Westies will slim down with an extra walk and a smaller portion of their regular diet. If your Westie is begging due to the decreased dinner, check with your veterinarian about adding some frozen green beans or canned pumpkin—plain, please—to his diet. These products add fiber without many calories. Most dogs like both of these items, and your Westie will feel full without any extra calories.

Make sure that you cut back on treats and don't give out any table scraps. Many round Westies manage to have "starving eyes" with bulging bellies! With a small-sized dog like the Westie, even one or two dog biscuits mean quite a few extra calories. Look for low-calorie alternatives, or distract your begging Westie with a rousing game of fetch.

Dogs don't always take kindly to going on diets, especially when their treats are involved. Studies have shown that dogs can count up to about five or six. So if your Westie normally gets two biscuits at bedtime, you are better off breaking one biscuit into two pieces and giving him the two treats. He won't notice that they are smaller, but he will be happy that he is not being "cheated"!

CHAPTER
**5**

# GROOMING YOUR WEST HIGHLAND WHITE TERRIER

**W**est Highland White Terriers naturally have an easy-to-care-for coat. It is harsh and coarse, with a soft undercoat below a layer of long, tough guard hairs. This coat stood up to rough and wet winters in the British Isles. Running through brambles and brushy areas naturally removed the old undercoat. Once dirt or mud had dried, a Westie with a natural coat could simply shake to cause almost all of the debris to fall off. Underneath would be a nice, almost dry, white coat.

For our pet Westies, coat care may be more complicated. If you choose to show your Westie in conformation or simply prefer the all-natural coat, you will need to learn to "strip" the dead hair out. If you simply want him clean and looking great, you may choose to have him clipped by a groomer to remove excess hair. This will soften the coat a bit, but your Westie will still look nice and have a bright white coat.

## GROOMING AS A HEALTH CHECK

Regular grooming will keep your Westie's skin and coat healthy. It will give you a chance to look for any parasites such as fleas or areas of irritated skin. Regularly putting your hands all over your Westie is like a mini-physical exam—you will notice any growths, any asymmetry in muscle, or any injured areas right away. Problems such as ear infections will be caught immediately, and you will prevent painful coat mats from developing.

Regular grooming will keep your Westie's skin and coat healthy.

## GROOMING SUPPLIES

You will require the following grooming supplies to keep your Westie looking his best:

- bath items: shampoo, cotton balls for the ears, dryer with a cool setting
- comb to detangle hair and for touchups
- dental care items: toothbrush, toothpaste, dental sprays or gels
- electric dog clippers if you choose to groom your Westie yourself
- grooming table so that you don't have to bend over
- nail clippers: scissors or guillotine type or a Dremel-type rotary tool
- pin brush to loosen any mats and brush out dirt
- scissors for trimming: thinning shears, straight scissors, and blunt-end curved scissors are all helpful
- slicker brush to remove dead hair and dirt
- stripping knife if you plan to leave the coat natural
- towels for drying
- wipes to clean the eyes and ears

Your Westie will need regular care to look and feel his best. Certainly once a week is the minimum for a thorough grooming. Dental care and a quick touch-up should be done daily. With regular care you will notice any changes in your Westie early and will help to keep his skin, teeth, eyes, and ears healthy. You will spot parasites or skin problems right away while they are easier to remedy. If you use a few treats and plenty of praise, you can make this a positive time for you and your Westie. Many dogs will solicit grooming because they enjoy the attention.

Save some of your Westie's favorite treats to use as rewards while you work on his grooming. You don't want him to get too round, but some tasty snacks may help him look forward to grooming sessions.

## COAT AND SKIN CARE

At least once a week, perform a thorough grooming of your Westie, including checking the armpits for mats and cleaning the area around the penis carefully if you have a male.

### BRUSHING

Your Westie will enjoy a quick daily pass with the pin brush or slicker brush.

1. Start by brushing gently in the direction of the hair from the head back to the tail.
2. Brush his sides from top to bottom after feeling for any mats or tangles.

3. Slicker down the legs and the tail.
4. Comb through the coat after brushing.
5. Check the armpits and behind the ears for any mats or tangles.
6. End by brushing the hair around the neck and head forward to achieve that characteristic "chrysanthemum" look.

All Westies will need serious trimming and touch-ups about every six to eight weeks. Pet Westies are generally trimmed or clipped on the back and neck areas and along the "skirt" on the sides.

## HAND-STRIPPING

Hand-stripping is a necessity if you choose to show your Westie, but some pet owners like the look and the texture of the coat as well. If you choose to hand-strip, doing a small amount daily is preferable to a marathon— for both you and your Westie. For hand-stripping or using a stripping knife, remember that your Westie will have hair of three lengths. There will be the new coat coming in, the healthy coat, and the older coat ready to come out. It is best if you have your Westie's breeder or an experienced terrier groomer help you get started on stripping your Westie's coat. You must identify the old hair that needs to come out, and you want to minimize any possible discomfort for your dog.

There is a knack to hand-stripping well. Some Westie lovers feel that it is

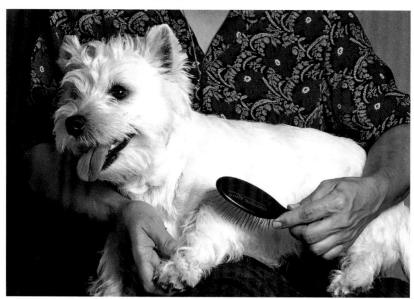

Your Westie will enjoy a quick daily pass with the pin brush or slicker brush.

## Dog Tale

Daryl Conner is a Master Pet Stylist and offers words of advice on bathing your Westie. "West Highland White Terriers are supposed to be white. Being low to the ground and of the temperament that getting into absolutely everything seems a good idea to them, sometimes they need a little freshening up. If you want to bathe your pet at home, look for a mild cleansing shampoo designed for pets. Whitening shampoos are available but should be used with care. Most whitening products contain a bluing agent. Because white is really an absence of color, the bit of blue laid on the hair shafts by the shampoo is designed to trick the human eye into perceiving a whiter white. If a bluing agent is overused, however, your white dog may possibly begin to take on a dingy gray color. Whitening shampoos can also be irritating to your pet's eyes, so if you do use one, be sure to keep it away from his face. Any time you wash your dog, remember this important tip: Rinse completely, then rinse again for best results."

therapeutic for both them and their dogs to enjoy some daily hand-stripping while watching television!

If you choose to finger-strip, you may want finger covers (like a file clerk).

1. Gently pull at a few hairs of the dead coat at a time. Hairs should pluck fairly easily.
2. With a stripping knife, the tool will separate out the dead hair.
3. Pull gently and move on to a new area.
4. Be patient—it is best to do a small area daily.

Westie clubs provide extensive charts in their educational materials that demonstrate how to hand-strip and will even give you a schedule of areas to rotate through.

### COMBO STRIPPING AND CLIPPING

Some families choose to do a combo of stripping and clipping called "strip-n-clip." This can be done by you at home or by a professional groomer. Normally when clipping your dog you will clip in the direction of hair growth. Make sure that your blades are sharp, and use plenty of lubricant. If you are unsure about doing any clipping yourself, pay your groomer to give you a lesson or two. It will be well worth it in the long run.

After combing out your Westie carefully and bathing him and drying him thoroughly, prepare to strip him.

When hand-stripping the coat, gently pull at a few hairs of the dead coat at a time.

1. Lightly strip the back, neck, and head.
2. Clip around the tail, and then switch to a smaller-sized blade. (Smaller numbers actually leave more hair.)
3. Clip the neck, back, and partway down the sides—you want to leave a "skirt" of slightly longer hair.
4. Carefully scissor by hand to trim your Westie's head, legs, and underside.

## BATHING

A Westie who is groomed regularly whether at home or at a groomer will rarely need a bath. Still, there will be times when your dog digs a major excavation or rolls in something smelly and you need to bathe him. Certainly if your Westie has a close encounter with a skunk, a bath will be in order. Check with his breeder for a recommended shampoo.

1. Organize your supplies first: shampoo, cotton balls to keep water from his ears, and towels.
2. Use a sink or tub with a nonslip mat.
3. Gently place cotton balls in his ears to keep water out.
4. Check the water temperature before you put your Westie in the tub—lukewarm is fine.
5. Gently wet him all over.

6. Apply a small amount of shampoo, mixing it with some water in your hand first.
7. Lather well, avoiding the eyes.
8. Rinse thoroughly.
9. Towel-dry as best you can.
10. Finish by air-drying or using a blower on low heat.

## The Anal Glands

The anal glands are small glands on either side of your Westie's anus. These glands should empty a bit each time your Westie defecates—they basically add scent to his "pile," saying "so and so was here." But sometimes the glands won't empty fully and can get blocked, so it's a good idea to check them periodically. You can ask your veterinarian or one of the veterinary technicians to show you how to do this. If your Westie goes to a groomer, ask to see whether the groomer checks the anal glands.

You can empty your Westie's anal glands at home—do this right before a bath. That way any debris that gets on his coat will be washed away. Take a thick tissue and hold that next to your Westie's rectum after you carefully lift up his tail. Gently put pressure on both sides of the rectum. If the anal glands are not empty you should get a watery yellow discharge or a slightly thick gray discharge. In either case, it will smell terrible. Dispose of the tissue and then get your Westie directly into the tub for his bath!

An important part of your Westie's daily care routine is taking care of his teeth.

## Skunk Encounter

If your Westie has had a close encounter with a skunk, use this recipe for best results: mix 1 quart hydrogen peroxide, 1/4 cup baking soda, and 1 to 2 teaspoons of liquid dish soap. Mix well and apply generously to your Westie. Let it sit

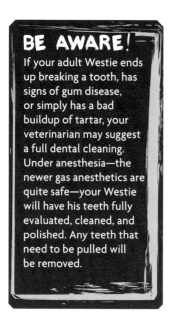

for about five minutes, then rinse thoroughly. Rarely might you need to repeat this. Perform this procedure in lieu of a regular bath.

## DENTAL CARE

An important part of your Westie's daily care routine is taking care of his teeth. After all, they need to last a lifetime! There are many dental care items that make it easy to keep your Westie's smile bright and white. Be sure to use dog-approved products, though—not human toothpastes, etc., or you could upset his tummy.

Start dental care with your Westie as a puppy by getting him used to your fingers near his mouth—without any biting! Putting some flavored toothpaste (chicken and peanut butter are favorite flavors) onto your finger and letting him lick it is a good first step. Then gently rub his gums with it. Next let him investigate and lick the toothbrush with some toothpaste on it.

To care for the teeth:

1. Brush daily with a special dog toothbrush, finger brush, or small soft brush designed for use on a child.
2. Simply slip the toothbrush inside the lip—there's no need to force his mouth open.
3. Then brush gently along the outside of the teeth. Your Westie's tongue helps keep the insides of the teeth clean.

Add a dental plaque fighter to your Westie's meals, and use a dental spray or gel daily after brushing.

## EAR CARE

Westies are fortunate to have nice prick ears that are well ventilated. Still, the ears can get infections, suffer from ear mites, or provide the first sign of a food allergy. You should set a routine of checking your Westie's ears at least once weekly.

If you notice him shaking his head, pawing at his ear, or holding his head with a slight tilt, check the ears right away. He may need a visit to your veterinarian. Also, if his ear suddenly tips at the end or has a swelling in any part of the ear

Fortunately, Westies have nice prick ears that are well ventilated.

flap, he needs immediate veterinary attention.

To care for the ears:

1. Gently pull the ear up straight so that you can carefully look inside. The skin inside the ear should be a healthy pink.
2. If you see any wax or debris, use an ear wipe to clean it out. Don't use a cotton swab, which may simply push the debris farther into the ear.
3. There should not be any discharge.
4. If your Westie's ear is red, inflamed, or painful, he needs to visit your veterinarian.

Caught early, ear infections are much easier to treat!

## EYE CARE

Your Westie should have bright eyes with no discharge. If he is squinting or has discharge, call your veterinarian. Eye problems can go from minor to serious very quickly.

Tearstaining can be diet related or caused by blocked tear ducts. If your Westie develops brown stains below his eyes, talk to your veterinarian for products to help.

Because Westies are small in stature and enjoy poking their heads into holes and animal dens, they may easily get dust or debris in their eyes. Also, the sensitive corneas can easily be scratched. If you participate in some of the active dog sports with your Westie outdoors such as earthdog trials or take long walks where he might get dust in his eyes, you may want to ask your veterinarian about a daily eye wash that is safe to use to flush his eyes in the evening and after those outings.

Check your Westie's eyes daily, noting that a normal eye will not have any discharge:

1. Look for redness, discharge, cloudiness, or squinting.
2. Watch to see whether your Westie paws at his eyes or rolls and rubs his face on the carpet or ground outside.

3. Flush with artificial tears if there is any debris.
4. Use an eye wipe to clean around the eye.

Contact your veterinarian if you see any signs of trouble.

## NAIL CARE

The very mention of trimming dog nails puts many people into a panic. However, with some care and patience, this can be a quick and easy routine chore for you and your Westie. A Westie whose nails have been neglected may develop a splayed foot and sore pads. Nails may actually grow around and into the pads, especially if your Westie has his dewclaws left on—vestigial nails and pads partway up his front legs. Long nails tend to get brittle and break or crack. Both of those situations can be quite painful.

Ideally, your Westie's breeder gently handled him while he was a puppy. If not, or if you have a rescue Westie who is a bit sensitive, you need to gently handle his feet daily. Simply hold the paw lightly for a second. Then give him a small treat. Once he tolerates that well, give the paw a gentle squeeze when you hold it. Most dogs are less fussy about having a rear foot touched, so you may want to start your nail trimming in the rear. If your Westie is fussy about his feet, simply try to do one foot or even one nail a day. Most Westies have dark or black nails, so you can't count on "seeing" the sensitive area, or the "quick," as it is commonly called. The quick is the

A Westie who mostly romps on lawns and soft grass will need more frequent nail trimmings.

Master Pet Stylist Daryl Conner has had numerous Westie close encounters. "He doesn't like to be brushed," Mrs. M. told me as she handed me her wiggling, squirming six-month-old Westie puppy Hank. He wasn't smelling springtime fresh, and his coat was starting to form some tangles. So Mrs. M. brought him to me to be professionally groomed. Knowing that Hank had a long life of brushing ahead of him, I invited his owner to come into the grooming area with me for a lesson on coat care. I put a safety loop around Hank's neck to remind him to stay on the table and showed his owner the most important two tools she would need: a slicker brush and a good metal comb. Hank did his part by throwing a very credible little temper tantrum. His owner was horrified. I assured her that her boy was just asserting his opinion and that our job was to show him the error of his ways. I waited until he took a breath and popped a really great little treat in his mouth. Each time he stood still for brushing he was rewarded with something delicious. In mere moments, Hank, being a smart boy, was standing quite still while we brushed and combed his coat. His first professional grooming was a success, and I hoped we'd have many happy appointments in the future.

sensitive area inside the nail where the blood vessels and nerves run. If you cut a nail too short, this area will bleed and feel sensitive for a day or so.

How often your Westie will need his nails trimmed varies with the individual dog. A Westie who takes long daily walks along a sidewalk will wear his nails down a bit and only need infrequent trims. A "country" Westie who romps on lawns and soft grass will need more frequent trimmings. You should check the nails weekly when you do a thorough grooming.

1. Have your clippers or rotary tool ready, along with some styptic powder in case you cut the quick—basically cut the nail too short—and it bleeds. Also have a treat or two on hand.
2. Hold your Westie still or have a helper gently restrain him. Petting and rubbing may make him forget all about his feet!
3. Pull the hair away from the nail. If you are lucky enough to have some white nails, you can see where the quick is.
4. Holding the foot level, figure that you can always safely remove the curve or the part of the nail that turns down from the pad.
5. This part of the nail will look like a "V" after you trim—if you see a circle, you are getting close to the quick.

6. Trim quickly. If you are matter of fact and confident, your Westie will relax.
7. If you use a Dremel-type tool to sand the nail down, be sure to check that it is not getting too hot.
8. Give him a treat and some quiet praise as needed while you trim.

If you accidentally cut the quick, do not panic. Simply stick some styptic powder on the end of the nail. It should clot quickly. Then keep your Westie quiet for a bit so that it seals over. A Westie with a bleeding nail can look like a disaster; every time he steps he may leave a spot of blood. It truly isn't very much, but spread around it can look frightening. So keep him quiet, and don't panic.

## FINDING A GROOMER

You may decide that it would be simpler to have a professional groomer work on your Westie's coat. That is an option that many families choose. Most groomers will groom a Westie in a "pet cut" using clippers. If you want your Westie maintained with the natural coat, you will need to find a groomer experienced in hand-stripping and willing to take on a terrier coat. If your breeder is nearby, she may be willing to help. If you plan to show your Westie in conformation, you need to either learn to hand-strip or find an agreeable groomer. But no matter

Most groomers will groom a Westie in a "pet cut" using clippers.

With a pet cut, Westies continue to look adorable!

how your Westie gets groomed, you want it to be a positive experience for him.

With a pet cut, Westies continue to look adorable. They won't have the slightly longer skirt of a natural coat and there will be less "ruff" to achieve the "chrysanthemum" appearance of the head. Still, the shiny white coat and bright eyes make any Westie a winner. Make sure that your groomer knows he is a Westie and not a light-colored Scottish Terrier. You may want to take some photos of Westies groomed the way you like when you go to the groomer. You can search online, look through Westie calendars, or take photos of friends' Westies done in a style you prefer.

Most groomers work out of independent shops, but some will function as part of a pet store or veterinary clinic. A few groomers make house calls, and that might be the perfect solution for you.

Finding a groomer means doing some homework on your part.

- Find out whether your Westie's breeder knows a good groomer in your area.
- Check at the local pet stores and veterinary clinics for recommendations.
- If you meet other Westie families out and about, see whether you like their dog's cut. If so, ask who their groomer is.
- Visit the grooming shop before your first appointment.
- Evaluate the shop in terms of cleanliness and safety for the dogs.
- If possible, bring your Westie by for a quick hello and a nice treat once or twice before his first appointment. You want him to think of the groomer's as a positive place.
- Discuss with the groomer exactly how you would like your Westie trimmed.
- Find out whether nail trims and anal gland cleanings are included.

# HEALTH OF YOUR
# WEST HIGHLAND
# WHITE TERRIER

In general, Westies are very healthy, hardy little dogs. Think back to your breed's origins as a farm dog living in harsh conditions. Most Westies go through life with few problems and are active well into their teens. Still, your Westie will need some veterinary attention, even if it is only well checkups and preventive care. An excellent reference for your Westie's health care is an e-book done by the West Highland White Terrier Club of America (WHWTCA). It can be found at www.westiefoundation.org/westiehealth/healthebook.htm.

## FINDING A VET

Finding the right veterinarian is important to you and your Westie. You need someone whom you are comfortable with, who listens to you, and who respects your opinions. You want someone who enjoys working with dogs and hopefully has a good rapport with your Westie. In addition, there are basic needs that every good clinic should fulfill.

• Is the clinic clean and neat?
• Is emergency coverage provided—either by that clinic or through an emergency clinic?
• Are referrals to specialists encouraged, or are there specialists in the practice?
• Is the clinic reasonably nearby and easy to get to?
• Is there emphasis on preventive and wellness care?

Finding the right veterinarian is important to you and your Westie.

For senior dogs, a twice-annual exam is a good idea.

- Are alternative therapies offered if you need or want them?
- Are there payment options if you need help covering an unexpected emergency?
- Are you comfortable with the way the staff and the veterinarians treat you and your Westie?
- If there are multiple doctors, are you comfortable with all of them? Of course you might have a favorite, but are you willing to see all of the doctors there?
- Can you get counseling on nutrition and behavior?

You may want to ask friends or neighbors which veterinary clinic they use. Your local animal shelter can also provide recommendations. If there is a local kennel club, ask at a meeting to see which clinic members recommend. You can also look online for listings of veterinary hospitals from the American Veterinary Medical Association (AVMA) and American Animal Hospital Association (AAHA). Don't hesitate to schedule an appointment simply to talk to one of the veterinarians and get a tour of the facility.

## THE ANNUAL VET VISIT

Even a Westie in perfect health should have an annual visit to your veterinarian. the vet will give your Westie a full physical exam—from snout to tail tip! Eyes, ears, and teeth will be examined for any potential problems. His heart will be evaluated and his temperature taken (probably not his favorite part of the visit). Your Westie's weight will be checked and your veterinarian will discuss his diet. Any necessary

## PUPPY POINTER

Keeping your Westie puppy in sight or confined will limit his chances of mischief and medical emergencies.

preventive tests such as fecal exams for parasites and blood work to check for heartworm and tick-borne diseases will be done.

Your veterinarian will go over any preventive medications your Westie needs, such as heartworm preventives or flea and tick preventives. Any supplements to keep your Westie feeling in tip-top shape will be discussed. A vaccination and care schedule will be customized for your Westie based on his activities, lifestyle, and where you live. A "city" Westie may not need leptospirosis vaccinations, whereas a "country" Westie who frequently encounters wildlife may need the vaccine.

For senior dogs (over seven years of age) a twice-annual exam is a good idea. Older Westies may need routine blood work to look for early signs of kidney or liver problems. Caught early, many of these problems can be managed fairly well. If there are any heart irregularities detected, your Westie may get radiographs (X-rays) or an EKG (electrocardiogram).

## SPAYING AND NEUTERING

Unless you are an experienced dog fancier and your Westie has not only passed all of his health clearances but also is a topnotch example of the breed, you really shouldn't get involved in breeding. A reputable breeder does an immense amount of homework before breeding, has found and screened puppy buyers before even doing the breeding, and is prepared to take back any dog or puppy she has ever bred. If you can't say yes to those stipulations, then simply spay or neuter your Westie and enjoy him or her as a fabulous family member. Most spayed and neutered dogs are better as all-around family companions.

Previously it was recommended that puppies be spayed or neutered at six months or even earlier. It is now felt that waiting until 10 to 12 months on a small-breed dog like a Westie may encourage more natural growth.

For spaying, generally the uterus and ovaries are removed. If this is done before your Westie ever has a heat cycle, you reduce the chances of her developing breast cancer by over 90 percent! Even after one heat, there is a great reduction in breast cancer risk. Plus you don't have to worry about stray males showing up when your Westie is in heat or having to deal with fending off suitors in your yard or on walks.

Neutered males have both testicles removed. This means that there is much less chance of developing prostate enlargement, as well as fewer behavior problems, such as roaming or marking inappropriately.

## VACCINATIONS

Veterinarians have come to look at vaccinations in a new way. Vaccination schedules should be customized for each individual pet. Which vaccines your Westie needs depend on many factors, including his age, health, travel plans, lifestyle, and activities. There are "core vaccines" that are recommended for all dogs. These are canine adenovirus (or canine hepatitis), distemper, parvovirus, and rabies, which is also mandated by the law. Other vaccines are either "noncore" but recommended for dogs in certain situations or not recommended at all because their efficacy is not ideal or the diseases they cover are readily treatable.

Puppies need a series of vaccinations to help them develop their own immunity as the immunity they got from their dam's colostrum (her first milk, which is rich in antibodies) wears off. This series generally starts at about 8 weeks of age and

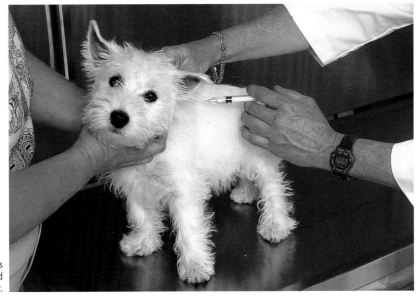

Vaccination schedules should be customized for each individual pet.

goes until 16 or 18 weeks of age with a booster once a month. The rabies vaccine is initially given anywhere from three to six months and may be dictated by state law. After a yearly booster, most dogs can be safely shifted to vaccine boosters every three years. This period of immunity may be extended even further in the future.

## CORE VACCINES
The following are some core vaccines that your Westie should receive.

### Canine Hepatitis
You may hear this virus referred to as adenovirus, but it is the same disease. The virus attacks the liver, kidneys, and blood vessel linings. In the acute form, the dog will die very quickly, despite care. Some dogs will recover with symptomatic care, including fluids and nursing care for the appetite loss, fever, and jaundice. A few dogs will end up with bluish-tinged eyes as a permanent result.

### Distemper
The name "distemper" is a misnomer for this disease. Westies with distemper are not bad tempered; instead they are very sick, and many of them will die. Signs include severe respiratory illness or vomiting and diarrhea. Some dogs will appear to recover and then develop neurologic signs like seizures. Some develop "hard

Not only is it the law, but given the prey instincts of your Westie, it is best to vaccinate for rabies.

pad disease," which is a form of distemper that leaves dogs with thick, crusty footpads and a crusty nose.

The vaccines for distemper are excellent, and your Westie should be vaccinated against it. This virus is present throughout the world and is a major killer of dogs. Dogs with distemper can respond to treatment, and some will heal with no residual problems. While there are no specific anti-viral treatment fluids, antibiotics for secondary bacterial problems and good nursing care may prevail.

### Parvovirus

Parvo is a deadly virus that attacks the hearts of very young puppies and the intestines of older puppies and dogs. This is another widespread disease, and dogs without protection are very susceptible to it.

A Westie with parvo will show vomiting and diarrhea, usually with blood involved and sometimes with very high fevers. Dehydration is common, and many dogs require hospitalization. Medications to control the vomiting and diarrhea, along with nutritional support, are important. This virus is quite hardy—another case where vaccination is the best option.

### Rabies

This is a fatal disease. The virus is present throughout the United States, and rabies cases have been found in cities as well as out in the country. Your Westie could even infect you, so this is called a zoonotic disease.

Your dog must be vaccinated against rabies according to the law. Dogs with rabies show one of two types of signs before they die. Some dogs get depressed and walk with a staggering gait. They are thirsty but have trouble drinking. Other dogs get the "manic" phase and act wildly and very aggressively.

If your Westie is exposed to a rabid animal and he has not been vaccinated or is not current on his vaccine, he will have to be quarantined. Given the prey instincts of your Westie, it is better to simply vaccinate against this! Dogs felt to have rabies should be euthanized; there is no treatment.

## NONCORE VACCINES

Three noncore vaccines that may be recommended for your Westie are those against bordetellosis, leptospirosis, and Lyme disease. Depending on your Westie's lifestyle and activities, these vaccines may be important for his health.

### Bordetella

This bacterium, *Bordetella bronchiseptica*, is associated with kennel or canine

The bordetellosis vaccine is most important for Westies who routinely go places where many dogs are present.

cough. These cough syndromes actually have multiple causes, including the parainfluenza virus. Very often dogs with these syndromes feel quite good but sound terrible, with a honking sort of cough. The cough may linger for months in rare cases, however, and some dogs will develop secondary pneumonias that can be life threatening.

The bordetellosis vaccine is most important for Westies who are going to be boarded, stay at a groomer's for the day, or routinely go places where many dogs are present—like day cares, dog parks, dog shows, etc. Many kennels actually require this vaccine. Treatment against *Bordetella* may be given as a nasal spray.

Dogs with kennel cough need to be given nursing care and kept isolated so that they don't spread the illness.

## Leptospirosis

This is another bacterial illness. Leptospirosis is commonly associated with infected urine from wildlife, although it can be spread from dog to dog and also from dog to human. Westies living in the suburbs with wildlife nearby are at risk for this disease, as are Westies living in the country. Dogs with leptospirosis show liver and kidney signs: jaundice, vomiting, muscle pain, and often fever. Treatment consists of supportive care, antibiotics, and good hygiene to make sure that no one else is exposed via infected urine.

Previous vaccines were not considered to be that effective and often caused reactions. The newer vaccines cover more serovars—versions of the leptospirosis bacterium—and are much safer and more effective.

### Lyme Disease

This is a tick-borne bacterial disease that is now quite common across the United States. Using intermediate hosts like mice and deer, the bacteria are spread through tick bites to dogs (and people). Clinical signs include fever, pain, swollen joints, and often kidney problems. Long-term antibiotics seem to keep this illness in check, but recurrences are common. This is mainly a disease of dogs who are in the suburbs and country and have tick exposure. Still, if you travel or if your city Westie competes in earthdog trials, you will need to take precautions. Depending on where you live and the risk of exposure, your veterinarian may simply recommend tick control or may suggest both vaccination and tick control. Remember, you need to customize the vaccination schedule for your individual Westie.

## PARASITES

Parasites can exist, during at least part of their lives, only by living on or as part of other living beings. Some of them can harm your Westie by draining nutrients. Others actually deliver serious illnesses and diseases. One of your

Lyme disease is a tick-borne illness that uses intermediate hosts like mice.

goals for your Westie's health care should be to keep him parasite-free. Many of these parasites are happy moving from your Westie to you, so the whole family should prefer no parasites!

## EXTERNAL PARASITES

External parasites exist on the outside of your Westie. This group includes obnoxious pests like fleas, mites, and ticks—as well as fungal infections like ringworm. Although some of these pests are fairly unusual parasites, others are quite common. Preventive medications may be suggested to keep your Westie free of them.

### Fleas

Fleas are rugged, athletic parasites, capable of running and jumping from victim to victim. Westies can be exposed to fleas from other dogs and from wildlife like squirrels and rabbits, and can even pick them up outdoors in flea-infested areas.

You may notice quick brown "bugs" running through your Westie's white coat or spot them when he rolls over as they run across his abdomen. You might even pick them up when you comb through his coat, especially near the tail area.

Dogs react to flea bites by scratching, biting, or chewing on the bitten areas. Some dogs will itch to extremes and have severe allergic reactions to the flea saliva. Badly chewed skin areas are open to bacterial infections. In addition to the coat and skin damage they cause, fleas can infect your Westie with tapeworms. Once fleas latch onto your Westie, they can then establish themselves all throughout your house.

There are now excellent topical medications that can be put on once monthly as needed to kill or even repel fleas. Flea birth-control

Check your Westie for fleas and ticks after he's been playing outside.

treatments can also be orally administered to your Westie.

If your Westie contracts fleas, treat all of your pets and be prepared to treat the house if necessary.

## Mites

A variety of mites can infest your Westie. Sarcoptic mange mites make dogs really uncomfortable with severe itching. These mites can come from your Westie's hunting habits, and squirrels are a common source. The mites are detected by skin scrapings at the vet's and require special treatment, including medicated baths and dips.

Another type of mite, *Cheyletiella*, is occasionally seen on puppies and looks like "walking dandruff"—its nickname. Flea baths and treatments work well for this mite.

Demodectic mange is caused by a microscopic mite that normally lives on dogs with no problem. However, these mites tend to manifest in dogs with immune problems. Puppies may simply outgrow a mild case, but adults infected with *Demodex* will require dedicated treatment with baths and dips.

Ear mites will rarely infest a Westie. These mites can be acquired from other dogs or from the family cat. If one of your Westies shows up with ear mites, check all of the other family pets. Ear mites require regular ear cleanings and medication to remove them.

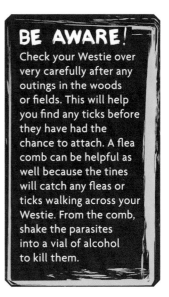

**BE AWARE!**
Check your Westie over very carefully after any outings in the woods or fields. This will help you find any ticks before they have had the chance to attach. A flea comb can be helpful as well because the tines will catch any fleas or ticks walking across your Westie. From the comb, shake the parasites into a vial of alcohol to kill them.

## Ringworm

Ringworm is a fungal infection that, true to its name, will cause red circular areas of inflamed skin on your Westie. These areas may or may not be itchy. There will be hair loss in the infected areas, and you can catch this from your dog, so practice good hygiene. If you have a cat, your cat or kitten may be the source of the ringworm. Treatment generally consists of medicated baths. Sometimes oral medications are needed.

## Ticks

Ticks are nasty parasites. They carry a number of severe diseases, including Lyme disease. Ticks are slow-moving and hang out on grasses or branches

If your Westie seems unusually lethargic or otherwise unwell, take him to the vet.

waiting for a good host to wander by—and your Westie out exploring is an ideal host. Ticks use intermediate hosts as well, ranging from birds to rodents or deer, depending on the exact tick species. Once on your Westie, they attach to feed on his blood and in return may give him one of the tick-borne illnesses. When attached, ticks hang on until they are bloated with blood. You may find them near your Westie's ears and neck, where they cling when he pokes his head into holes to explore.

Tick prevention has come a long way, with most veterinarians recommending monthly topical medications or possibly special collars. If you find a tick on your Westie, remove it using gloves or a handy tick-removal tool and bring it to your veterinarian for evaluation.

## INTERNAL PARASITES

Internal parasites are organisms that live in your Westie—again, draining nutrients and possibly causing other diseases. Some of them may infect people as well, so clearly, preventing them should be a high priority in your Westie's care.

### Heartworms

Heartworm is a serious mosquito-borne disease that literally leads to large worms living in your Westie's heart and lungs. Heartworm has been detected all across the United States, so your Westie should go on a monthly or daily heartworm preventive. Treatment involves the use of arsenic compounds and can be dangerous. This is definitely a disease that is better to prevent than to treat!

### Hookworms, Roundworms, and Whipworms

Hookworms, roundworms, and whipworms are all intestinal parasites that can drain nutrition from your Westie. A heavy load of these parasites can make a Westie puppy anemic and may even cause death. Hookworms and roundworms are contagious to people, so good hygiene is important if your Westie is diagnosed with one of these parasites. You should bring a fecal sample for evaluation on each of your Westie's veterinary visits. Treatment is generally fairly straightforward with a dewormer. Daily "poop patrols" are a good idea so that your Westie doesn't reinfect himself. He can be born with these parasites or pick them up from contaminated ground.

### Tapeworms

Tapeworms can infest your Westie from one of two sources. Fleas, as well as mice and other rodents, can carry tapeworms. So if your Westie has a bout of fleas or is out hunting, you may find tapeworm segments (which look like dried rice) around his rectum. Tapeworms are treated with oral medications.

## WESTIE-SPECIFIC HEALTH PROBLEMS

In general, Westies are quite healthy and long lived—most live into the double digits, often reaching 12 to 15 years of age. Still, there are some diseases to which Westies appear to have a genetic predisposition. That does not mean that all Westies will have these problems or even that most Westies will; it simply means that these problems are seen in the breed. The WHWTCA participates in the Canine Health Information Center (CHIC) program and recommends hip, patella, and eye certifications for all Westies used for breeding.

## ATOPY

"Atopy" is the word for inhalant allergies. A Westie with atopy will breathe in certain pollens or other allergens and then itch, lick, bite, or chew on his skin. You may notice saliva staining on your Westie's feet or face from licking and chewing. Some Westies will develop secondary bacterial or fungal infections on the inflamed skin.

Intradermal skin testing is recommended to determine exactly what your Westie is allergic to. If it is something as simple as feathers, you can eliminate feather pillows from the house. Generally, Westies have multiple allergens,

A Westie with copper toxicosis should be medicated and put on a low-copper diet.

however. Symptoms can be controlled with anti-inflammatory medications and helped by fatty acid supplements, but dogs often get worse with time. Desensitization with injections is often the best course of action.

## CATARACTS

Cataracts may be seen in young Westies. They should be removed surgically once they are "mature." Cataracts can predispose your Westie to glaucoma and also interfere with his vision. The CHIC eye exam will detect early cataracts in your Westie.

## COPPER TOXICOSIS

Copper toxicosis is related to a genetic defect in how your Westie's body handles copper in his diet. From puppyhood until about four years of age, copper can build up in the liver. Over time, signs of liver failure become apparent: weight loss, loss of appetite, vomiting, pain in the abdomen, and eventually jaundice. A biopsy provides the accurate diagnosis. Westies with copper toxicosis should be put on a low-copper diet and given medications to prevent copper from being deposited in the liver. With care, many of these dogs lead normal lives.

## CRANIAL MANDIBULAR OSTEOPATHY (CMO)

CMO is a genetic defect that affects Westies, along with Scottish Terriers and Cairn Terriers, emphasizing their common background. At about three to four months of age, families notice that their Westie's lower jaw is thickening. This is not a cancer. The added bone can make it painful for your Westie to open his mouth, eat, and drink. Anti-inflammatory medications do help. Luckily, the condition starts to resolve on its own at about a year of age in most Westies. Some Westies will even end up with a normal jaw. Most others will be comfortable and able to eat and drink with no problems.

### LEGG-CALVE-PERTHES DISEASE

Legg-Calve-Perthes is an autosomal recessive genetic defect. Parent dogs may appear normal, but their puppies can develop a necrosis of the femoral head and neck. This means that your Westie has a serious problem with one or both of his hind legs, and you may notice limping or pain. This condition is diagnosed by radiographs (X-rays). If your Westie has this problem, surgery is the best treatment. Mild cases can be managed with rest and medication, but arthritis will develop. This problem will be caught through the Westie CHIC program.

### PATELLAR LUXATION

A luxating patella, or loose kneecap, can be a hindrance to an active Westie. You may notice your Westie doing a "skipping" gait or holding up a hind leg now and then. The patella slippage is found on gentle palpation by your veterinarian. Surgery is recommended to tighten up the ligaments and prevent the development of arthritis. Early diagnosis is important. This is one of the problems the Westie CHIC program tests for.

### PULMONARY FIBROSIS

Pulmonary fibrosis, or Westie lung disease, results from lung tissue scarring. This condition generally shows up in older Westies, about ten years of age or more. The first signs may be a cough or a decrease in exercise tolerance. The problem seems to have a genetic basis but is also affected by environment. Medical therapy helps and should

**Dog Tale**

"Sprite" was the perfect name for the cute, bright-eyed Westie puppy, but her movements weren't sprightly. She was lame and felt pain. Sprite was a puppy mill puppy, purchased from a pet store. She had bilateral Legg-Calve-Perthes. Luckily, she was diagnosed early; with surgery, she went on to lead a normal and active life.

be started early to minimize secondary heart problems.

## WHITE SHAKER DOG SYNDROME

White Shaker Dog Syndrome is a problem of the nervous system. Affected puppies start with body tremors any time from five months to three years of age. Tremors seem to increase with excitement and stress. Some Westies even have trouble walking because the tremors are so strong. This problem has been seen in other white breeds such as Maltese. Anti-inflammatory medications and muscle relaxants may be used as treatment.

Herbal therapies actually form the basis for many of our "standard" medications.

## ALTERNATIVE THERAPIES

Alternative therapies are treatments outside standard "Western" medicine. Some, like acupuncture, have science behind them and are almost mainstream. Others are more exotic. Make sure that any alternative practitioner is certified to treat pets—in fact, it is best if that practitioner is a veterinarian. In many states it is illegal for nonveterinarians to treat pets unless under the direct supervision of a veterinarian.

### ACUPUNCTURE

Acupuncture uses carefully placed needles to stimulate energy meridians in your dog. It has been shown to be effective for various types of pain such as arthritis and for helping with some chemotherapy side effects.

### CHIROPRACTIC

Chiropractic involves the manipulation of joints to relieve stresses on various body parts. Your Westie should have a thorough physical and possibly even X-rays before any spinal manipulations. You don't want to make an existing condition worse!

## HERBAL

Herbal therapies actually form the basis for many of our "standard" medications. But it is important to realize that simply because an herb is "natural" does not mean that it is safe. Herbs can be dangerous or even deadly. Deal with a veterinarian who is knowledgeable and certified in the use of herbs. Make sure that she is aware of all medications and supplements your Westie is already taking. You don't want to have a bad drug interaction!

## HOLISTIC

Holistic simply means looking at your Westie from a "whole" point of view—his environment, his lifestyle, his diet, etc. Any dedicated veterinarian will take all of those things into consideration when treating your Westie.

You should have a pet first-aid kit at home, ready and assembled for use.

## FIRST AID

Basic first aid is important for your Westie. You can assume that at some point he will get into mischief that may cause a minor injury or two. Many local Red Cross affiliates now offer classes in pet CPR and pet first aid. These are worthwhile classes for you to take.

You should have a pet first-aid kit at home, ready and assembled for use. You can purchase kits or make one yourself inexpensively. A small plastic container to hold everything is ideal. Have cards with important phone numbers such as your veterinarian, nearby emergency clinic, and an animal poison control center. Keep an up-to-date copy of your Westie's vaccination and medical records in there, along with a list of his diet, medications, and any supplements he's taking.

Items for a basic first-aid kit include:
• adhesive tape (to hold bandages on)
• antibiotic ointment (after wound cleaning, can heal a small cut)
• cold pack (can handle a bee sting)

Older Westies may show some signs of slowing down.

- diphenhydramine (Benadryl—can handle a bee sting)
- disposable gloves (so that you don't touch infected areas or parasites like ticks)
- eye wash solution (to flush any debris that gets into your Westie's eyes)
- hydrogen peroxide (to induce vomiting if needed and recommended by poison control)
- liquid bandage (can help with a scraped footpad)
- roll gauze (to use for bandaging or to make a quick muzzle)
- scissors (to cut tape and bandage materials)
- sterile gauze pads (to place next to wounds and for cleaning)
- thermometer (can be digital or rectal)
- tweezers (to remove splinters, ticks, etc.)
- wound-cleaning solution (chlorhexidine or betadine)

## THE SENIOR WESTIE

In general, Westies remain hardy and healthy into their teens. Still, an older Westie may show some signs of slowing down. Arthritis is common due to the active lives most Westies lead. Many older Westies can be made comfortable with joint supplements such as chondroitin and glucosamine. Others may need prescription anti-inflammatories to be comfortable. Discuss your options with your veterinarian.

Changes in vision and hearing are common. Even with cataracts, most older Westies can get around quite well because they have a "mental map" of your home and yard. Just don't rearrange the furniture! A Westie who is going deaf may still be able to hear a high-pitched whistle or a clap. You can also stamp your foot when you approach a sleeping older Westie. The vibration will waken him so that he isn't startled when you touch him.

Many older Westies will have some urinary incontinence. This means that you have to be more vigilant about getting him outside frequently. Use easy-to-wash pads or blankets on his bedding so that you can keep everything clean. You may need to crate your older Westie at night to prevent him from wandering and to help with urinary leakage. Talk to your veterinarian about medications that may help.

Some older Westies may develop canine cognitive dysfunction (CCD). This is similar to old age dementia in people. Your Westie may seem disoriented, have trouble with commands he has always known, and develop problems with housetraining. There are medications you can ask your veterinarian about to help with this.

It is important to maintain your senior Westie in good condition. He should be at a good weight and in decent shape. While you may have to shorten the length of his walks, he still needs regular exercise. Ensure that he is getting a good-quality diet as well. It can be tempting to spoil your senior citizen, but hold firm and stick to foods he should eat.

In general, Westies remain hardy and healthy into their teens.

# TRAINING YOUR WEST HIGHLAND WHITE TERRIER

Training your Westie should be a wonderful part of your bond and your partnership. A trained dog is welcome in many places, and the training journey will help you to understand and appreciate each other. And training is, or should be, fun! Remember, your Westie is clever and quick witted.

A trained Westie is a companion who is welcome to go places with you like pet stores, dog parks, and friends and relatives' homes. A trained dog is always welcomed with pleasure at the veterinarian's office and the groomer's salon. A trained dog who has passed the American Kennel Club's (AKC) Canine Good Citizen (CGC) test may even get you a discount on hotel stays and homeowner's insurance. A trained Westie has many options to explore with you: therapy dog work, obedience, rally, agility, tracking, freestyle, and earthdog. Without training, your Westie will often be left at home, alone and crated.

## POSITIVE TRAINING

Positive training means helping your Westie to understand the task and giving him some incentive, motivation, or "pay" to want to do that task. Dogs who are trained with positive methods tend to be enthusiastic and willing partners. You can use treats, toys, or simply time with you as positive reinforcement for your Westie. You will need large doses of humor and patience because most Westies are clever beasts with goals of their own and an independent streak. You will also need to be creative and firm because your Westie will do his best to manipulate and train you!

Positive training does not mean that your Westie will never know what a correction is. Dogs learn best with a combination of praise for doing the right thing and a correction or distraction to mark what is not acceptable behavior. A "correction" may range from simply ignoring the behavior to a distraction with a "no" or a sharp noise. A good trainer will foresee problems and distract the

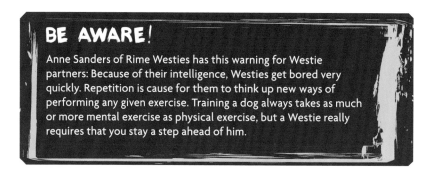

**BE AWARE!**

Anne Sanders of Rime Westies has this warning for Westie partners: Because of their intelligence, Westies get bored very quickly. Repetition is cause for them to think up new ways of performing any given exercise. Training a dog always takes as much or more mental exercise as physical exercise, but a Westie really requires that you stay a step ahead of him.

When positively training your Westie, use praise and treats to reward him for a job well done.

Westie before the problem happens. A Westie will learn best with consistent and fair black-and-white rules about behavior. Don't fall for that cute face and ignore "badness."

Many trainers use a clicker (a small metal noisemaker) as a marker to let their dogs know when they have done the correct thing. You can achieve the same effect with your voice by saying "Yes" or "Excellent" or whatever word you choose. Both methods will work, so do what is most comfortable for you. Concentrate on your timing so that you "mark" the behavior you want at the exact moment your dog performs it. Follow your marker with a reward of some type.

One more tip: Don't set up a training session when you are tired or not feeling well. You need to be able to focus 100 percent on your Westie. If you act as though training is a chore, he will see it that way too. Instead, it should be a fun time for the two of you to enjoy together.

## SOCIALIZATION

Socialization is the exposure of your Westie to everything and anything in his world. Ideally, socialization will continue for your Westie's entire life, with you frequently exposing him to new adventures and things. A dog who lives in isolation can easily become aggressive and very wary of anyone or anything new.

Balance socialization experiences with your health care. Until your pup is fully covered with his vaccinations, plan your social outings carefully. Visit friends with dogs who are friendly and healthy. Avoid dog parks or places with many strange dogs. Carry (instead of walk) your Westie in to your veterinary clinic for a quick hello, some petting, and a treat. Set up situations at home with different flooring, tapes of unusual noises, and mini-obstacle courses.

## HOW TO SOCIALIZE

As mentioned previously, great socialization means exposure to a variety of experiences, people, other dogs, noises, different footing, etc. At all times, you want these exposures to be positive experiences. Bring good treats for new people to fuss over your pup when he sits nicely. Use treats to encourage him onto a new type of footing, or toss his favorite toy onto it.

*Socialization is the exposure of your Westie to everything and anything in his world.*

If something startles him, steady him, then back up to a point where he is comfortable. Gradually approach again, stopping whenever he hesitates. Do not act as if it is a big deal or it will become a big deal in his mind. Quit when you are ahead and plan to re-expose him to that obstacle another day.

## Places

You can do some socialization at home. For example, set up different types of footing for your Westie. Use a shag rug, a tight-weave rug, and linoleum. Concrete flooring in the garage is a new experience, as is the wood floor on your deck. Play different types of music, and on occasion put nature videos or action shows on the television. You can build a "tippy" board using a small piece of plywood with a tennis ball attached to the bottom. Your Westie will quickly master the wobbles!

A miniature dog walk can be constructed of a plank set on two bricks. Then move up to cement blocks for supports. Garage sales can be great sources for children's tunnels and sturdy plastic playhouses with mini-slides, doorways, and windows. Let your Westie explore these on his own. These exposures will all build his confidence. If you have an adult Westie, he will help the puppy in new situations, providing a sturdy anchor if your pup gets concerned. For example, agility tunnels are fun for all terriers, and Westies are no exception. If your adult Westie whips through the tunnel, the pup is sure to be close on his heels.

If you live in the country, try to take your Westie to a safe place to walk with asphalt or concrete pathways. Let him hear traffic noises. Conversely, if you have a city Westie, make sure that he gets to some parks for outdoor experiences. Running through safely fenced wooded areas means that he will be exposed to leaves, logs, and possibly even a creek.

Many pet stores as well as farm stores and some hardware stores will allow dogs to come inside. Your pup will be exposed to many great scents, new flooring, and usually some dog-friendly people. At first your Westie may be most comfortable riding in the cart—that is a new experience too!

## People and Dogs

Socialization means getting your Westie puppy out to meet people of all sizes and ages, including people with hats, people with beards, people with skirts that blow in the wind. It means introducing him carefully to children, infants, and toddlers. It also means exposing your Westie to other dogs—but choose friendly

If you live in a more rural area, try to expose your Westie to more urban sounds, like traffic noises.

Think of the crate as your Westie's den or bedroom.

dogs! A puppy class can be a great place for your Westie to mingle with other puppies and with puppy-friendly people.

If you are thinking about doing therapy work with your Westie, expose him to wheelchairs, walkers, and crutches. Always make sure that he is safe and not frightened. He may even enjoy a short ride on someone's lap in a wheelchair.

Watching local school sports events can be great socialization. Your Westie will hear cheering, see people dashing about, and probably hear some squeals of childish delight. The announcer is another unique exposure. Bring treats for people to feed him when he sits quietly.

## CRATE TRAINING

Used properly, a crate can be a lifesaver. It will also provide you with a safe place for your Westie when you travel or if you have holiday company. Think of the crate as your Westie's den or bedroom. It is his private space. It should not be a place of punishment for him, and he should not spend many hours every day in it away from the family.

Many Westies will arrive at your home with some crate experience. Most breeders expose their puppies to crates, and most adult dogs, either rehomes or rescues, will have been crated. Try to have something from the breeder or foster home in your crate—a small towel or blanket is a good choice. You want familiar smells for your Westie, who may be feeling a bit overwhelmed.

## HOW TO CRATE TRAIN

Initially have the crate door open and simply toss a treat or toy into the crate. Your Westie will bound in and probably bound right back out fairly quickly. This is fine at first. When he is comfortable going in and out, shut the door just for a second or two. Many dogs will simply lie down in the crate to enjoy their treat. Others may throw temper tantrums. If your Westie throws a tantrum, do nothing. Simply wait until he calms down and is quiet. Then open the door.

Repeat this procedure off and on throughout the day. The crate should start looking like a positive place to be. For a nap or bedtime, placing a safe chew toy with treats into the crate can be a good idea. Make sure that it is a hard rubber toy that your Westie can't chew up. Remember, if he throws a tantrum, you have to be tough and wait it out.

# HOUSETRAINING

Housetraining and crate training tend to go hand in hand. Your Westie has no desire to eliminate in his own bedroom, although he couldn't care less about your imported rug.

There is a general rule of thumb for puppy bladders: Figure that your Westie puppy will need to go outside every two hours if he is two months old, every three hours if he is three months old, etc., up to six months of age. Most puppies can wait longer during their overnight sleep, but that is a good schedule for during the day. Ideally, your Westie should never have to go more than six hours during the day without a walk.

## HOW TO HOUSETRAIN

Dogs prefer to be clean if given the choice. When your Westie fusses in his crate after a rest, he probably needs to go outside to pee. Take him right out and praise him when he goes.

You may want to designate a certain area of the yard for your Westie's elimination. If so, always carry or take him right to that spot when he wakes up or shortly after he eats or drinks. Any time your pup circles or stops after a bout of playing, get him outside. Initially figure that within ten minutes after he eats or drinks, immediately when he wakes up after a nap, and right away if he stops while playing, your Westie will need to go out. Also, if he is circling and sniffing, he probably needs to go out.

How long will it take to housetrain your Westie? Partly it depends on how long it takes your Westie to train *you* when to take him outside! Most breeders start housetraining with their litters by having a separate area in the puppy pen or room for elimination. The puppies quickly learn to go over in that corner and keep their main area clean. Still, expect some accidents and be prepared with an enzyme cleaner to completely eliminate the odor to keep your puppy from wanting to go there again. Do not punish him for an accident—*you* are the one who missed the signs and didn't get him out in time.

## BASIC COMMANDS

Basic obedience can help your Westie to become a model canine citizen and good neighbor. If you investigate the AKC's CGC program, you will see that knowing how to sit, down, stay, come, and walk nicely on a leash are all important parts of its certification.

A well-behaved dog is welcome in many places, from hotels to friends' houses to outdoor cafes. In addition, a well-behaved dog makes your life easier. You are less stressed since you aren't constantly worrying about what your darling Westie is about to do. Your Westie is calmer since he knows his training and his boundaries.

Before you start any training, make sure that everyone in the household is on the same page as to commands and proper performance. If one person says "Sit" and another person says "Sit down," your Westie will be confused. It isn't fair to him for people to be inconsistent. If necessary, keep a list on the refrigerator with your Westie's command words. You can add to the list as he learns new things.

## Dog Tale

Sandy Campbell of Camcrest Westies has this to say about training: "Westies have a way about them that makes them unique. They have no small amount of self-esteem, which many owners and admirers can tell you. Westies are not for everyone, but if you are the type of person who loves to be entertained, loves a challenge, and don't expect obedience, then try a Westie. Always keep in mind when training the Westie that the command needs to be his idea and he doesn't work for a pat on the head—he wants something out of it, like a treat. They don't like coddling unless it is their idea. They are a man's dog, bred to hunt, and that is what they love to do. They are your best friend and will be at your side wherever you want to go. They are your partner, your buddy, your friend, and your love."

*Sit* is a position that gives you a bit of control and reminds your Westie to exercise some self-control.

## SIT

*Sit* is a very important skill for your Westie to learn. It is a position that gives you a bit of control and reminds him to exercise some self-control. Imagine waiting at the veterinarian's office with your Westie zooming around at the end of his leash, jumping on and off the seating. Now picture him sitting quietly by your feet. Both of you are much calmer in the second scenario.

*Sit* can also be used for your Westie to earn his "benefits." Make him sit quietly before you let him outside. Have him sit before you put his food bowl down. Ask him to sit to greet people. Your Westie is well on his way to being a good citizen.

*Sit* is also an easy trick for any dog to learn. This is a position dogs assume naturally, so you know that your Westie can follow this cue!

### How to Teach *Sit*

The easiest way to teach the *sit* is with a tasty treat. Have your Westie on nonslippery footing like carpet or grass outside in a fenced-in area. If he tends to wander off, you may want to have him on lead.

Show him the treat, then raise the treat just above and a touch behind his head. He will automatically sit to raise his head. As the head comes up, the rear should go down. Say "Sit" and give him the treat. If he tries to stand up on his hind legs or jump up, simply close your hand over the treat and start again. If you ask your Westie to sit this way three or four times a day, he will have this mastered in less than a week. Then start to wean off the treats, giving him a food reward only at random times. Never forget the praise, however!

Like the *sit*, the *down* is a nice control position.

You may decide to add a hand signal to the verbal command. That can be fun and will keep your intelligent Westie on the alert and paying great attention to you.

## DOWN

The *down* position can be a bit harder to teach. From your Westie's point of view, this is a submissive posture. Most Westies aren't thrilled about that. Also, your Westie realizes that from a *down* position it will be harder for him to suddenly take off to chase a squirrel or do other fun things. Just remember, every Westie can and does lie down at some point during the day, so you know that he can do this.

### How to Teach *Down*

It is nice to have a slippery floor to teach this command. Have your Westie sit first. Then take a treat and bring it down to the floor and back between his front legs. Most dogs will slip into a *down* to get the treat. You can also do this from a stand if you can get your Westie to stand still! Do not get into a wrestling match with him. He may forget his manners and make a quick grab with his teeth because he doesn't have hands to push back with.

If you notice your Westie starting to lie down on his own, quickly say "Down" and head over to hand out a nice treat. He can use the *down* position to earn rewards too. A quick *down* when you walk in and he has muddy feet means that you can easily wipe his feet off and reward him with a treat! He can down as you open the door or down next to the table while you eat. Like the *sit*, the *down* is a nice control position.

## STAY

Once your Westie has mastered *sit* and *down*, you should add a *stay* command. "Stay" means that your dog remains where he is, in the position that he was told to take, until he is released. Many people use "okay" or "free" as their release words. When you use the release word, your Westie will quickly learn that he is now free to get up and move around.

### How to Teach *Stay*

It is easiest to teach *stay* if you have your Westie in his buckle collar and on a lead to teach this cue. Tell him to sit or down and then add the word "stay." It really helps to add a hand signal to this command. So as you say "Stay," put your hand, palm toward him, in front of your Westie. The hand adds a physical barrier and reminder that he is to remain where he is. Your leash can hold him back if he goes to move away.

At first you should expect your Westie to stay only for seconds and only with you right there in front of him. Gradually you can add time and then distance. Eventually, your Westie should be able to stay for a minute or more with you at the end of your 6-foot (2-m) lead.

## COME

Coming when called, or the *recall* as it is called in formal obedience, is very important for your Westie. A quick *recall* could even save his life if he is heading toward a busy road. This is also one of the hardest commands for your Westie. If he is busy sniffing his way after an interesting scent or is about to take off after a squirrel, he really has no desire to come to you. One of your goals is to make yourself so interesting and worthwhile that your Westie chooses coming to you over other fun activities. There will be times, however, when you will lose out to his instincts, so try to always have him in a safe area if he is off lead.

### How to Teach *Come*

You can start teaching your Westie to come with fun puppy games. Have one

Coming when called could save your Westie's life one day.

member of the family gently restrain him while another person runs off a short way. That person should then turn and call him. Most puppies won't be able to resist a quick chase to "catch you." Once he reaches you, reward him. Then prepare to send him back to the original holder. Puppies love this game!

Once your Westie is a bit older and has learned to sit and stay, you can tell him to stay, go to the end of the lead, and then get down and call him. If he doesn't come, you can gently reel him in. Remember to reward him when he gets to you. If your Westie is loose in the yard, you can call him and then run the other way. Once again, most Westies can't resist a fun game of chase and catch.

It is important to have the word and the action of coming always associated with positive things. So if your Westie hates to be groomed, don't call him to be brushed. Quietly go and get him instead. Don't always call him and then bring him in from the backyard. Make it a habit to call him, give him a treat, and then let him go back to playing sometimes. That way he'll think of coming as a good interaction between the two of you, with a nice payoff for him.

## WALKING ON A LEASH

Even if you live on a farm, there will be times when your Westie will need to be on leash and walk with you. Every Westie should learn some leash manners. Good leash manners mean that he is not jerking your arm out or twisting around your legs. He must pay attention to you. When you stop, he needs to stop. If you have to speed up or slow down, he should do so too.

### How to Teach *Walk Nicely on a Leash*

Westies who live in the city or suburbs get early leash education. After all, they have to walk

## PUPPY POINTER

If your back bothers you when you lean down to train your Westie puppy, there are solutions. You can do *sit* and *down* training on a grooming table. Once he knows the commands, simply transfer your Westie's training to the ground. For leash walking and providing rewards, a long-handled cooking spoon with a mashed treat works wonders to keep him focused and your back from aching.

to eliminate. You can start with your puppy by simply letting him drag a leash around while you are there to supervise. Once he is accustomed to the leash, you can begin to pick it up and follow him. Your Westie will now think of the leash as a nice incidental item that brings you together.

Next, your Westie needs to learn to go with you on the leash. It is a good idea to have some treats handy. Encourage your dog to come with you with the promise of a treat—held out like the carrot before the proverbial donkey. If he takes two or three steps cheerfully with you, reward him. Most Westies catch on to this quickly and will march along, waiting for their treats. Use a command like "With me" unless you are teaching formal heeling with strict precision.

Most Westies walk nicely on a leash around the yard, in quiet places, or down the hall inside. The difficult part is getting them to also walk nicely when things get exciting outdoors. Always try to have some treats with you to distract your Westie from temptations like squirrels. Just be sure to hang your jacket up high back at home so that your pockets don't get chewed out by a Westie on the hunt for crumbs.

It is nice to give your Westie a chance to check out smells and lead the way on occasion. Many trainers give their dogs a word that means "you are now free to check things out." It might be as simple as your release word used after your Westie has walked nicely for a while. Or you can choose a word that specifically means "this is your time."

Following your Westie can be an eye-opener for you as well. He'll notice plenty of things that might have escaped your eye: a lost penny, an interesting bug, or a spring flower just peeking up through the snow.

A well-trained Westie is a joy to have as part of the family.

## Troubleshooting

There are a couple of things you can try if your Westie insists on pulling. One is the "be a tree" method. When your Westie pulls, you stop. Simply stand quietly. Eventually it will occur to him that you are no longer moving. Most Westies will then glance back at you and relieve the tension on the leash. Once the tension is relieved, start forward. The minute he pulls, stop again. This requires a great deal of time and patience on your part, but it also works very well if you are consistent. Westies are smart, and they quickly figure out that to get what they want (going forward) they need to do what you want (keeping the leash loose).

Another helpful method is to simply turn and go in a different direction when your Westie is pulling full steam ahead. It is best if you do this with no warning— simply turn and move off on your own. Your Westie will have no choice but to follow. Your path may be erratic as you dance and dart in different directions, but this forces your Westie to pay attention to you.

## FINDING THE RIGHT TRAINER

Finding the right trainer to help you move beyond basic commands at home can be a challenge. The ideal trainer has Westies or at the very least a terrier breed. Such individuals may be few and far between. Ask for recommendations from your veterinary clinic, your groomer, the local pet store, your local shelter, and friends who have done training classes with their dogs. Many areas have obedience clubs that offer classes in the evenings and sometimes during the day. Go and watch classes at a couple of places. Attend an obedience trial and watch for local dogs who are upbeat and happy working in the ring. Ask people competing with their terriers whether they can recommend an instructor.

Here are some things to look for when you check out classes:

- Is the facility clean and neat?
- Do the dogs and handlers appear to be enjoying themselves?
- Is the instructor positive and upbeat?
- Does the instructor offer multiple ways to teach new exercises or just one?
- Does the instructor customize the teaching to each student?
- Are you comfortable with the methods being used?
- Are health clearances required?

Make sure that your instructor is comfortable with you occasionally taking your Westie off for a break. While many dogs like sporting breeds can handle multiple repetitions, your Westie will not. He will quickly get bored and then start to get creative. This is generally not a good thing! Most instructors are adaptable as long as you don't disturb the class. Simply take your Westie outside for a quick breath of fresh air and a potty break, or quietly take him to the side and let him play a game of tug.

A basic obedience class is a good option for almost every Westie. It will help to continue his socialization and help him learn to focus even with distractions. It also means that he gets your dedicated attention, all to himself, at least once a week.

After obedience class, you may find your Westie sacked out and snoring on the drive home. Concentrating in class can be both mentally and physically exhausting for your bundle of nonstop energy!

# SOLVING PROBLEMS
# WITH YOUR
# WEST HIGHLAND
# WHITE TERRIER

It is always better to prevent problems than to fix them later, but sometimes your Westie either comes with a problem behavior or has learned one despite your best efforts. It is important at all times to remember how much you love your West Highland White Terrier and think of the joy his companionship brings to you. Most problems are surmountable, although it may take time and effort on your part.

What is a problem behavior? This is actually an intriguing question. What constitutes a problem behavior in your eyes may be a perfectly natural behavior from your Westie's point of view. You are horrified that your Westie just dug up a full bed of your imported tulips. Your Westie is incredibly proud of himself for catching the vole that was hiding among the flowers. You see lost money and hours of wasted work. He sees himself as a doggy hero who just saved the family. There are also behaviors that may be a problem for you, such as barking at squirrels from your apartment window, and that also bother your neighbors. Meanwhile, a friend in the suburbs is thrilled that her Westie barked and scared off a vandal. Barking is a behavior that is totally natural to your Westie, but you may need to put controls or brakes on it.

Some behaviors need to be trained away or modified. For other behaviors, it may be simpler to modify *your* behavior or your routines. For example: Your Westie, who is good as gold otherwise, gets into your trash when you are at work.

If you wish to change a behavior, such as your Westie's unwanted sitting on your nice leather couch, you must catch him in the act.

It may be simpler to put the trash where he can't get at it than try to booby trap the trash can, catch him in the act, etc.

If you wish to change a behavior you must catch your Westie in the actual act. Finding the trash strewn about the floor hours later and throwing a fit won't have any meaning to him. It is also often best if you can arrange a correction/distraction without your obvious involvement. That way, your Westie won't behave like an angel when you are around and let the devilish side of his personality out when you are away.

It may take many, many repetitions to establish a correct behavior in your Westie's mind. Be prepared to make that effort to strengthen your relationship. It is worth it to eventually have a hassle-free companion.

## PUPPY POINTER

Debbie Duncan, a longtime Westie fancier and trainer, offers these insights:

"Some owners are unprepared for the Westie's big-dog vocalizations. Terriers have large and intimidating voices, which are designed to convince larger dogs, animals, and predators that they are fierce and a force to be reckoned with. Even their puppy play growls can sound fierce to the untrained ear."

## BARKING

Barking is a natural behavior, and all dogs bark to some extent. What you want is to control your Westie's times and urges to bark. First, you must remember that Westies were selected for barking; a sharp, loud bark let the farmer know where the Westie had cornered the vermin. The bark had to carry even if the dog was underground in a den. That is a lot of bark for a small dog!

### HOW TO MANAGE IT

Step one is not to encourage your Westie to bark. If a game gets a bit wild and he starts to bark, stop the game with a "Ssshh." Wait until he has calmed down a bit before playing again. You must be consistent! Every time you fudge and let him bark a bit, it is reinforcing to him. Some dogs simply like to bark.

Your Westie may be barking when he looks out the window and sees a squirrel running across the yard. If you work away from home, it may be easiest to just close your Westie out of rooms having window access to where squirrels are likely to be. With some treats, chew toys, and his crate to nap in, he may be perfectly happy in a laundry room with one high window and the door blocked off with a baby gate.

If you are at home, you can decide whether you will let him have one bark and then call him to you, tell him how brilliant he is, and reward him for now being quiet. Or call him to you right away—no "free" barks. Just make sure that you take the time and effort to reward your Westie when he is being quiet. Often people forget to reward the "good" behaviors because they aren't annoying and attention-grabbing.

Although terrier barking is almost always associated with hunting or alarm barking, it can develop out of loneliness. No Westie should be left alone for long periods every day. These are social little dogs who enjoy being around people.

## CHEWING

Chewing is another very natural behavior for a dog and especially so for a puppy who is teething. Your Westie enjoys chewing his food and chewing on his play toys, so why not chew on your shoes? To begin with, people's possessions do tend to smell strongly of the person who owns them. To a dog, those odors are a powerful attractant. If your beloved human isn't around, he's thinking at least he can pacify himself by chewing on something that smells like you.

Your Westie may be a small dog, but he has the jaws and teeth of a much larger dog. Terriers have strong jaws for grabbing vermin, pulling them out of dens, and then fighting with them. You should expect your Westie to want and need to chew. The goal is to direct his chewing to acceptable targets.

Remember that your Westie won't be able to discriminate between an old shoe and a new one. Using old shoes or items of clothing as toys will simply encourage him to chew inappropriate items. Don't encourage him to chew sticks either or he may develop a fondness for table legs. As always, prevention is easier than treatment or retraining later.

Some Westies will chew inappropriate objects all their lives, but many settle down on the chewing habit as they reach adulthood.

# Dog Tale

## HOW TO MANAGE IT

Step one is to provide your Westie with plenty of good chew items. This might include fresh marrow bones—long enough so that they can't get stuck in his jaw. Hard rubber toys generally stand up to Westie chewing quite well. These toys can have treats, kibble, or sticky pastes put inside to encourage your dog to chew and lick even more. Solid rubber balls make good play toys and also stand up to chewing quite well. Discuss the use of rawhide chews with your veterinarian. Some dogs do not handle rawhide chews well, and you don't want to harm your Westie. Because of contamination concerns, use only rawhides made in the United States.

Step two is to put the things you don't want your Westie to ever chew safely away. That means that the expensive shoes should be behind closed closet doors. You can put bitter-tasting sprays on table legs and chair rungs to discourage chewing.

Step three is to make sure that your Westie is not left unsupervised until he is past the primary chewing stage—usually by about one year of age. Keep him with you or safely secured in his crate, a kennel, or an ex-pen.

Some Westies will chew inappropriate objects all their lives, but many settle down on the chewing habit as they reach adulthood.

## DIGGING

Of course your Westie will dig—he is, after all, a terrier! This is what terriers were designed and bred to do—dig out vermin from dens in the earth. His sturdy legs, strong nails, and determined attitude all contribute to a well-made digging machine. For your Westie, digging is perfectly natural.

Obviously, you may not have the same joyous outlook on digging as your Westie does, but realize that it is an ingrained part of his instincts. This is another

Give your Westie an alternative place to dig to keep him from uprooting your flowers.

case where it makes more sense to try to find an outlet for your Westie's instinctive behaviors as opposed to squashing them.

## HOW TO MANAGE IT

There are excellent resources, such as Cheryl Smith's book *Dog Friendly Gardens, Garden Friendly Dogs*, that give directions on building a "digging pit" for your dog. A blocked-off area with sandy soil where you can hide some chews or treats will encourage your Westie to put his paws to use there. You can hide new items daily, including toys and older bones.

Combined with the digging pit, you need supervision to stop your Westie the minute he thinks about digging elsewhere. If you can consistently stop him and take him to "the pit" with something good hidden, you will convince him that the pit is the place to be. This also means that you need to be vigilant about your yard. If you have moles or chipmunks, you will need to set traps to remove them. Otherwise, your Westie's instincts will kick in and he will dig them out for you.

Check around the perimeter fence at least weekly. Along with your Westie digging out, you could have rabbits digging in. Either way, that area will attract your Westie and stimulate his urge to dig. Some families pour a small concrete lip around the bottom of the yard fence or put some chicken wire or sturdy mesh down to discourage digging.

If you try the sport of earthdog trials with your Westie, he will learn when and where it makes sense to dig. Many dogs enjoy the sports that are instinctive for them. This also gives your Westie an approved outlet for expression of his instincts.

## HOUSE SOILING

If your Westie suddenly starts having accidents in the house, your first action should be to schedule a veterinary visit to rule out any health problems. Take a fecal sample and also a urine sample if possible. The first urine of the morning is the best for testing. Along with obvious illness problems like parasites, diabetes, bladder infections, or kidney problems, also consider things like arthritis. If your Westie is having trouble going up and down stairs to go outside, he may simply be sneaking off to another room to urinate. Your veterinarian will look at his complete physical and medical history, as well as do a thorough exam.

If you resort to yelling at your Westie for house soiling, he may begin to hide it.

### HOW TO MANAGE IT

Accidents with young Westies or recent rescues usually stem from being given free run of the house too soon. Your Westie won't want to mess in "his area"—his crate, ex-pen, or kennel area. He probably won't mess in the areas he generally shares with you either. However, a rarely used guest room may not come under his radar as part of "his" space. You should go back to basic housetraining. Follow a schedule for eating and drinking, along with set times to go outside. Remember to praise him fully when he does go outside. Be more vigilant about observing him so that you notice right away if he goes to circle or heads for the door.

Make sure that you are not expecting too much of your Westie. If you get up in the morning, give him a quick walk, feed him, and dash off to work, you can't expect him to last another eight hours without a walk. Perhaps you can arrange for a neighbor to let him out at midday. A dog walker who comes on days you know you will be late coming home can be a wonderful arrangement. Perhaps you know a responsible teenager who would love to walk and play with your Westie right after school. Westies in the prime of life can be continent for many hours, but young dogs and senior canine citizens need relief breaks frequently.

Male Westies may show "marking" behavior—usually urinating on vertical surfaces to let everyone know that "they were there." This problem tends to show up around puberty, anywhere from 6 to 18 months of age. Neutering generally stops it. If you wish to keep your boy intact, you will need to be vigilant. If you don't let him out of your sight, you can distract him and get him outside the moment he raises his leg. Many male Westies seem to mature out of the need to leave urinary graffiti. Expect a possible resurgence if you add a new canine member to the family or possibly during times of stress.

Remember to clean any soiled areas with enzyme cleaners—not ammonia. Ammonia mimics the smell of urine, so your Westie might feel that it is okay to urinate there again. It is no use scolding your Westie if you find the mess after the fact. He won't connect the scolding to the mess. Plus it is actually your mistake for not observing him closely enough.

## JUMPING UP

Jumping up is a bad habit that many Westies are allowed to develop. Dogs love to greet their friends with a face licking and eye contact. That is difficult to do when you are a small dog! Dogs who jump up may scare people who are afraid of dogs to begin with. They may tear nylons or put dirty paw prints on nice outfits.

Jumping up is a bad habit that many Westies are allowed to develop.

Small children can be knocked over by a vigorous Westie jumping to greet them. In addition, if your Westie is leaping up on his hind legs and slips, he could hurt himself as well.

## HOW TO MANAGE IT

It is best if your Westie never has a chance to learn this habit. Right from the start, tell people that of course they can pet your cute Westie puppy but only when he has "four on the floor." This means that your Westie has to be standing or sitting to earn some attention.

Many breeders start this training off right when the puppies are in the ex-pen adjoining their whelping box. Visitors are told not to pet the puppies until all four feet are on the floor—so no petting the pushy puppy who is jumping up or has his paws on the side of the pen. It is hard to resist, but you must be consistent to establish good habits or break bad ones.

You will need to be consistent to develop good habits and prevent this behavior. You can't allow your Westie to jump up on you when you are in your weekend sweatpants and expect him to sit quietly when you are in your suit for work. You also can't expect him to know that it is okay to jump up on your teenage nephew but not your elderly grandmother. Better to err on the side of caution and simply not allow jumping up at all.

Once your Westie has this habit, it can be very difficult to break. Allowing him to do it even once in a while will help sustain the habit. You can start by having him on leash when he is going to greet people, either at your door or on the street. It is a good idea to set up some training situations. For example, as soon as someone approaches, tell your Westie to sit and stay. The minute he goes to bounce up, use the leash or his collar to hold him down. Remind him with the commands to sit and stay. You can have the person he is greeting offer him a treat when he is sitting quietly. The person he is greeting can say

Having your Westie sit when guests arrive is a good alternative to jumping up.

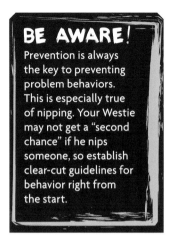

"Ah ah!" if he goes to jump up as well. That should distract him and remind him that this is not correct behavior.

Once your Westie has mastered the quiet *sit* to greet people, remember to reward that behavior off and on. People tend to forget to reward the good behaviors simply because they are good and not as noticeable. Even a gentle pet on the head or a scratch under the chin would be appreciated.

## NIPPING AND RESOURCE GUARDING

Nipping or biting is another perfectly natural dog behavior. If you watch two Westie puppies playing, it can sound vicious. They mutter, growl, and grab each other. Still, if it gets too rough, one pup will shriek and the play will stop for a minute. Then the puppy who was overwhelmed will often walk away, ending the fun. Prevention is the key to keep your Westie from ever developing the nipping habit.

With our litigious society, you can't afford to have your Westie give a person even a playful nip. You have to teach bite inhibition and reinforce it to teach your Westie good manners. Remember how big and strong those jaws and teeth are for a small dog. You don't want to be in court defending your Westie!

The dam of a litter of Westie puppies starts teaching bite inhibition herself right in the whelping box. This is why it is important to purchase a Westie puppy from a reputable breeder. Reputable breeders make sure that their puppies stay with the dam long enough and get proper socialization.

If your Westie seems to show true aggression and is willing to go beyond a nip, you may need some professional help. That means beyond your local obedience instructor unless that instructor is trained in animal behavior. An aggressive, unpredictable dog is not safe around your family and often is not a happy dog because he feels forced to defend himself so vigorously.

Always rule out physical problems with a dog who suddenly becomes aggressive or bites. An older Westie who has become arthritic may turn to snap if he gets rubbed roughly on his back. A Westie who is going deaf may snap in surprise when awakened from a deep sleep. Your veterinarian can do a complete physical and blood work to rule out health problems.

## HOW TO MANAGE NIPPING

Once your Westie puppy comes home with you, it is your responsibility to continue to reinforce good behavior and discourage any nipping. Do not play games where you tease him with your hands or your feet. All of his hunting instincts will come to the fore and he will grab with his teeth. This is also why you need to be sure that your Westie will trade or stop if you play tug with him. Never let him win. You must control the games.

Puppies have very sharp teeth, and their canine teeth curve backward. This means that even a casual nip might tear the skin badly. This is especially true of elderly people and people on certain medications. Be certain that your Westie has learned his manners before he encounters people outside his immediate circle of friends and family.

## HOW TO MANAGE RESOURCE GUARDING

Many Westies will "guard resources" such as food and toys. It is best to stop this behavior the second you notice it. Many human bites come from interactions over food or toys. This is especially true with children.

You should be able to come up to your Westie while he is eating and touch his bowl without having him react. If he does react, next time feed his dinner to him piece by piece from your hand. Or put one kibble in the bowl, have him eat it,

Many Westies will "guard resources" over food or toys.

then put the next one in, etc. This should help him realize that a hand near the food bowl is a good thing.

With toys, it may be simplest to do "trades." If your Westie has your shoe in his mouth, first, shame on you for leaving the shoe where he could get it! However, you do need your shoe back. This is not the time to start a tug-of-war. Instead, get another toy that your Westie likes or a great treat. Offer him the trade, then take your shoe off to safety. If your Westie gets highly attached to a toy and starts to growl if you come near when he has it, that toy needs to be removed. Offer a trade of another toy or a really good treat. Once you have the toy he was guarding so vigorously, put it away.

Good basic training can help prevent many problem behaviors.

One way to work with resource guarding is the "nothing in life is free" plan. Under this regimen, your Westie must earn every treat, privilege, etc. If he comes up to ask for a walk, he must sit or down before you put the leash on. He must sit or down and wait at doorways while you open the door. He must perform a behavior or a trick before he gets fed or petted. No more sleeping on the bed or cuddling on the couch. You must be consistent, firm, and fair at all times to straighten out his behavior.

Many dog bites are to children, especially boys around ten years of age. At that age, kids move quickly and often with accompanying shrieks and noise. Toddlers also take a fair share of dog bites. For them, the noise is most likely the inciting factor, along with food or toys held at an attractive height for a dog. It is a lot to expect a dog bred for hunting to ignore movement and high-pitched sounds. For that reason, some Westies with high levels of instinct simply should not be around children. A crate with a chew and a closed door are excellent ways to handle visits of young children for the Westie who is not comfortable with kids.

Most Westies can learn self-control and with supervision will be fine around well-behaved children. It is a two-way street, with both groups needing control. Your Westie may also adapt readily to your own children and accept their noise and movement. However, if friends are over or a birthday party for ten five-year-olds is planned, it might be best to provide your Westie with a quiet sanctuary.

## WHEN TO SEEK PROFESSIONAL HELP

If your Westie is truly showing aggressive behavior—attacking without reason, doing serious resource guarding that you can't deal with, or has bitten or seriously attempted to bite someone—you need help. As mentioned, first have a thorough veterinary exam done to rule out physical causes for pain.

The next step is to find a certified behaviorist. There are veterinary behaviorists and also trained nonveterinary professionals—many of them Certified Applied Animal Behaviorists (CAAB) through the Animal Behavior Society (ABS). There is also the International Association of Animal Behavior Consultants (IAABC). These groups all require training, certification, and continuing education in the field of animal behavior.

Nonveterinary professionals may work with a veterinarian if they feel that behavior-altering medications would be helpful. Even if medications are used, virtually all behavior cases require effort, time, and patience on your part to modify the behavior. Aggression and biting are taken very seriously.

Remember, prevention is much simpler than trying to fix problem behaviors. Start off on the right foot and help your Westie be a good canine citizen.

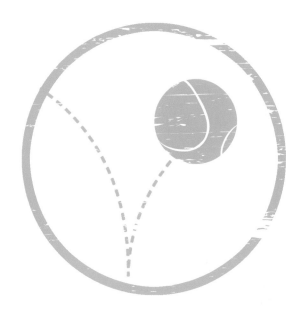

# ACTIVITIES
# WITH YOUR
# WEST HIGHLAND
# WHITE TERRIER

**W**esties are dogs who are often in action. They love trying new things, learning tricks and skills, and simply "doing." There are many great dog sports and activities that you and your Westie can try together. Most families find at least one sport that they and their dog enjoy.

## DOG SPORTS AND ACTIVITIES

Before heading into any dog sport, it is important to have basic control over your Westie and a sense of teamwork for the two of you.

### CANINE GOOD CITIZEN® PROGRAM

A great first step is trying the Canine Good Citizen (CGC) program. The Canine Good Citizen is an American Kennel Club (AKC) certification showing that you and your dog are prepared to be good neighbors. Many communities offer classes to help you prepare and train for this testing. The testing is done on lead and with a certified evaluator.

To pass a CGC test your Westie must accept a friendly stranger coming up to you and must sit politely for petting—so no barking and no wild jumping up! You are allowed to remind him of his manners if need be. He should also allow a person to touch him, groom him lightly, and pick up his feet. Of course, if your Westie goes to a groomer or has been socialized at your veterinarian's, this should be easy.

It may be harder for your Westie to walk on a loose lead, especially among a group of people. Westies tend to be sociable and curious, so you may need to remind your dog to pay attention to you. Basic obedience is also tested. Your Westie must sit and down on command and then stay in place until you call him.

Your Westie will also be judged on his behavior when someone with a neutral dog approaches you and on how he handles distractions like someone running by or a dropped pan. These distractions can be the most difficult tests for an alert terrier. He will want to bark and go to investigate. Lastly, your

## PUPPY POINTER

Your Westie puppy should not do any jumping for agility, obedience, or rally until he is fully grown. The growth plates in his bones (where the long bones grow from the ends) won't close until about a year of age. Before that time, they are easily damaged, and a damaged growth plate could mean a permanent orthopedic problem. He can play at running through tunnels, though!

Agility is a great sport for Westies because it is physical, fast, and fun.

Westie must show that he will behave if you hand his lead to someone and go out of sight for three minutes. Picture you needing to have someone stay with him while you dash off to a nearby bathroom, for example.

Your part of the CGC is signing the pledge to take care of your dog's health, exercise, training, and quality of life.

## AGILITY

Agility is the exacting dog sport in which dogs race over obstacles, fly over jumps, run through tunnels, and weave through poles. You may have watched agility competitions on Animal Planet on television. Agility is a great sport for Westies because it is physical, fast, and fun.

While it may look as if the dog-and-handler team is barely communicating while running an agility course, they are actually closely tuned in to each other. Many agility instructors require prospective students to take an obedience class first to show that they have control and that their dog is comfortable around other dogs and able to listen even with distractions. A Westie who is going to be doing agility should also be checked to be sure that he does not have any orthopedic, vision, or hearing problems that might interfere with his enjoyment of the sport.

Agility is a sport that can be physically demanding. Climbing up and down an

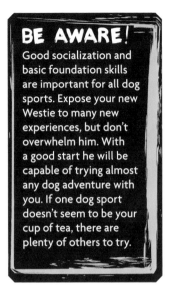

A-frame puts a strain on your Westie's front end. Jumping requires good vision and sound joints. Still, Westies are sturdy, energetic dogs, and this sport fits them well.

To run agility, the dog-and-handler team must follow the course as laid out by numbers. They must not knock down any bars on jumps, and they must honor the yellow contact or safety zones on the equipment. It takes focus and training to be able to do all of this—and while running.

For many Westies, the tunnels are the high point of the course. In fact, you will hear Westie competitors speak of "tunnel suck"—as if the tunnels were giant vacuums sucking their cute white dogs into them and off course!

You will need patience and a sense of humor to do agility with your Westie. He will tend to add extra tunnel runs to his performance, he may suddenly leave the ring to pursue a child walking by with a hot dog, or he may suddenly start sniffing or digging in the ring. Remember, he is off lead and he is an independent thinker and hunter by nature!

## CONFORMATION

Conformation, or dog showing, is what you see on television at the National Dog Show, Eukanuba, or at Westminster. Of course, those are big shows, and in some cases are by invitation only, but smaller shows open to young dogs and unfinished champions are found in most areas of the United States all year round. The original goal of dog shows was to choose the best breeding stock. Accordingly, only intact or unspayed females and unneutered males are eligible for conformation. Your male Westie must have both testicles descended into his scrotum.

For conformation showing, your Westie should be from a reputable breeder and must have no or only minor faults according to the breed standard. Temperament is important as strangers (the judges) will be evaluating him and putting their hands over him. He will also have to be comfortable around crowds of dogs and in noisy situations. A conformation Westie will have to be carefully groomed, including hand-stripped.

For conformation showing, your Westie should be from a reputable breeder and must have no or only minor faults according to the breed standard.

Not every Westie is cut out to be a conformation champion. Still, he can be a champion of your heart even if he doesn't fit the blueprint for the breed exactly.

## COURSING ABILITY

The newest AKC dog sport is coursing ability. This is a form of lure coursing adjusted to fit all dogs. Because most Westies are 12 inches (30.5 cm) in height or lower, they will run a 300-yard (274.5-m) course, chasing after a white plastic lure. The course is in a rectangular or "U" shape, with no turns of less than 90 degrees. A Westie must cover the course in one and a half minutes or less and follow the lure. Of course, to a Westie, chasing a "prey" animal is just plain fun. Two Westies were among the very first dogs ever to earn the AKC Coursing Ability title: Rivendell's Bea Dazzled RE JE with N. Sankus and Lonoch's SayGoodnite Gracie, also with N. Sankus.

## EARTHDOG TRIALS AND AMERICAN WORKING TERRIER ASSOCIATION TRIALS (AWTA)

If your Westie had the chance to design his own dog sport, it would be earthdog trials. Earthdog trials are set up for small terriers and Dachshunds. A tunnel is dug into the ground with twists and turns—all safely stabilized. At the end, there is an opening to place a rat safely ensconced in a cage. Your Westie has to scent the prey and then descend into the tunnel or den, barking at the prey to indicate that he has found it.

At the higher levels, the tunnel gets longer, has more twists and turns, and even has blind ends. Your Westie will be started from farther away and will have to scent his way to the tunnel entrance, and he will have to work with a partner dog.

Obviously, this sport was designed to show off the inherent hunting instincts in your Westie. He may resemble a cute stuffed animal, but he is actually a skilled

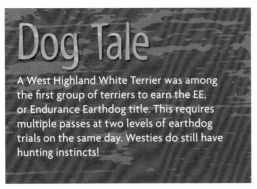

# Dog Tale

A West Highland White Terrier was among the first group of terriers to earn the EE, or Endurance Earthdog title. This requires multiple passes at two levels of earthdog trials on the same day. Westies do still have hunting instincts!

and tough hunter. The rat is safe in his cage, so your Westie can experience the thrill of the hunt without the risk of anyone getting bitten or hurt.

Just like the AKC, the AWTA offers different levels of achievement as well. The Certificate of Gameness means that the dog went into a 30-foot (9-m) earthen tunnel to reach his quarry within 30 seconds of release without help from his handler other than the initial command to work.

Working terriers may also earn credit for actual work hunting and dealing with pests on a farm as long as it is witnessed. But for trials, safely caged rats are used so that no animals are harmed.

## FREESTYLE

Freestyle, sometimes called "dancing with dogs," is another fun activity for Westies. You are encouraged to be positive and upbeat while training and competing. Many Westies seem to enjoy music and find the different moves interesting. It is another "active" sport, keeping your Westie on his toes at all times. Generally a dog will compete with just his handler, but there are divisions for pairs and teams.

Music choice is left up to you and your Westie—so you won't be limited to a bagpipe serenade. Some freestyle competitions are geared more toward "obedience to music," while others are truly "freestyle" with many different moves encouraged. Westies are a great size for weaving through your legs, and they can spin and twirl with the best.

Many Westies enjoy freestyle because the handlers are allowed to interact with their dogs more than in some other dog sports. Through

The active Westie enjoys a variety of sports and activities.

A Westie who participates in sports and activities will work off much of his excess energy.

quiet verbal commands or deft hand signals, you can help guide your Westie and encourage him.

## OBEDIENCE AND RALLY

Like the CGC, obedience and rally can be starting points for other dog activities. Both sports require you and your dog to work as a team with your Westie focused on you. Obedience is a bit more formal than rally and requires precision in your tasks.

At the lowest level of obedience, your Westie must walk in position at your left side first on a loose leash and then off lead. He must sit when you stop without being told to and change pace with you. He has to allow a judge to examine him with you 6 feet (2 m) away and come when called across a ring. Your Westie does all that in the ring with just you and the judge. The final test requires him to stay for one minute in a *sit-stay* with a group of dogs while you are across the ring and then stay for three minutes for a *down-stay* too.

In obedience the judge scores you for any imperfections in your performance. You need a sense of humor to show in obedience with your Westie. The minute the lead comes off, his terrier instincts may kick in. He may take off to chase the bag blowing by the ring outdoors or start digging at the site of a mole tunnel. He will always be a crowd pleaser, but you have to accept that on some days your exquisitely trained dog may have other priorities.

In upper levels of obedience, your Westie will have to work off lead but he will get to retrieve, jump, and do exercises that are much more exciting than merely heeling. A Westie who was bored with beginner obedience may really start to shine at upper levels.

Rally also requires you and your Westie to perform certain exercises, but in rally you are allowed to praise your dog and even pat your leg to encourage him if need be. In obedience the judge gives the commands and they are fairly standard. In rally you follow a numbered course that has different exercises for you to do. Westies seem to enjoy rally and do very well at it. Each competition has a different course, and Westies enjoy the variation as well as the extra praise they get.

## THERAPY WORK

Many therapy dog groups use the CGC as part of their evaluation procedure. They add in some tests to make sure that your dog has what it takes to go beyond simple good behavior and truly be tolerant of many people and strange situations. A *leave it* command is necessary to keep your therapy dog from snarfing up dropped medications in a nursing home or hospital. Your therapy Westie must be comfortable around wheelchairs, walkers, and crutches. Therapy dogs must also be tolerant of an occasional tight hand on their coats or an accidental ear or tail grab.

Some therapy dogs are more comfortable working with children, while others enjoy senior citizens. If your Westie has what it takes to be a therapy dog, you will find that you are in great demand. Everyone loves a Westie!

## TRACKING

Tracking is a sport that seems designed for Westies but with a caveat or two. In tracking, your Westie will be asked to follow the scent of a specific

To be an effective therapy dog, your Westie must be comfortable around all kinds of people and objects.

person and locate any and all articles that person may have dropped along the way. As you advance in difficulty, the track age gets older, the track gets longer, and you have more obstacles to deal with. Still, your Westie works in a harness and on a long

# Dog Tale

The first Westie to earn a Champion Tracker title, and in fact the first terrier of any breed, was CT Quicksilver Girl OA NAJ JE with Allison Platt on October 6, 1999.

line, so there is no possibility of a quick dash off on his own pursuits. You will be outdoors, which is the sort of place most Westies enjoy being. They have a great sense of smell, as they were selected to hunt and find certain game, even underground and in tough conditions.

The caveat is that your Westie *must* follow the scent of a specific person. If a squirrel runs across your track, your Westie must have the self-control and training to ignore it and concentrate on the scent he was told to follow. If mice dance through the tall grass alongside the track, your Westie must ignore them and stay on his track. The ability and skills to track are all present in your Westie in abundance; it is the self-control and focus that will take time to teach.

Many Westies do enjoy tracking—perhaps because it is one sport where the dog is in control. Humans are sadly lacking in scenting abilities, so we have to simply trust and follow our dogs. Just be prepared that your Westie may occasionally lead you on a merry chase.

## WESTIES HIT THE ROAD

Westies are wonderful dogs to travel with. They are small, their white coats suggest cleanliness (and no doggy odors), and their cute faces and outgoing personalities tend to endear them to fellow travelers. No matter what mode of travel you choose, your Westie can go with you and enjoy all the fun!

### CAR TRAVEL

If you expect to travel with your Westie in the car, it is a good idea to accustom him to it right from puppyhood. It may take some experimentation to figure out how he is most comfortable.

Dogs are safest traveling in a sturdy crate. The crate should allow your Westie to stretch out comfortably but not be so big that he could be flung around if you had to stop suddenly. Some Westies do better in a plastic crate with less visual stimulation, while others enjoy a wire crate so that they can see out. As a last

Although you might want your Westies to sit up front with you, they are much safer strapped into the back seat.

resort you could use a very sturdy tent or mesh crate, but these do not provide much protection in case of a crash. Regardless of type, the crate should be tied down in the car so that it won't roll or flip.

With your Westie in a crate, you need to consider airflow. You want him to be comfortable and free of drafts but still getting some cool air or heat, depending on the time of year. Check the airflow with your car running but stopped so that you can get out and put your hand by the sides of the crate to feel the air. It is a good idea to have a fixed water bowl in the crate. If your Westie tends to play with his water, you may want to freeze some in the bowl ahead of time or simply put in some ice cubes. They will melt slowly, providing him with water to drink but not enough to play in.

Most Westies appreciate a pad on which to lie. While yours is still a puppy, you may have to limit any cushy bedding, however, as a bored Westie pup might quietly chew, rip, or even eat some of the bedding during a long car ride. A foam-type cushion for the bottom of the crate covered with a fake sheepskin blanket that he can arrange to his satisfaction often works out very well.

For short trips, you may want to try a doggy seat belt for your Westie. These are not as safe as a crate but are much better than having your Westie loose in the car. The doggy seat belt goes on your Westie like a harness and is then clipped into the people seat belt. Do not let him ride in the front seat. If the airbag were to deploy, he could be killed. Also, never leave your Westie unattended in the car while in a seat belt. It is possible that he could get badly tangled or even strangle himself.

You need to prepare your car for having a dog along with you on trips. Make sure that you have a spare collar and leash. Plenty of baggies for poop pickup are a necessity. There are neat baggy holders that clip right onto the outside of your crate so that you can always find one quickly. Also, bring a container of water from home for him to drink to prevent tummy upset. If the trip will be overnight or longer, you will need to pack his daily food, along with any supplements or medications he takes.

You should have a copy of your Westie's rabies certificate and vaccination papers handy. The glove compartment is a perfect place to store them. Many parks and some motels will require them. If your Westie has any medical problems, you may want a medical history card with pertinent information in case you need to take him to an emergency clinic. Be sure that your Westie has his ID tags on his collar and that his microchip is registered in case he gets lost.

Westies are great travel companions because they are so portable.

## AIR TRAVEL

Luckily, your Westie should be small enough to fit into a traveling crate or sherpa bag under your seat. If at all possible, you want to avoid having him travel in the cargo compartment. Not all airlines welcome pets, and even those that do usually limit the number of pets allowed in the cabin on a flight. Be sure to make your reservation well in advance so that you know you can travel together.

Make sure that your Westie

is comfortable traveling in his crate and that he will rest quietly for a long time. Most airlines will not allow pets to come out of their traveling carriers even to sit on your lap. You can offer him water by carefully unzipping the top a bit. Providing a chew for takeoffs and landings to help his ears equilibrate is a good idea.

Depending on where you are flying and which airline you use, you may be required to provide a health certificate and copies of his vaccination records. Also, remember that he will count as one of your carry-ons, so pack accordingly.

## PET-FRIENDLY LODGING

There are many pet-friendly motels now, most of which accept dogs, especially if they are small like your Westie. Motel 6 offers a pet discount if you use the AKC code CP542764. Most Red Roof Inns are pet friendly, as are many La Quintas, Days Inns, and Comfort Inns. Still, always call ahead to be sure that the hotel you plan to stop at does allow pets.

Do not leave your Westie loose or alone (unless allowed) in a hotel room. If you leave him, he should be in a crate—this is where a tent or soft-sided crate is

Many vacation destinations are Westie-friendly.

There are many pet-friendly motels now, most of which accept dogs, especially if they are small like your Westie.

wonderful for an older crate-safe dog! If he tends to howl or bark if left alone, you will need to take him with you.

It is important to make sure that you and your Westie are model citizens when staying at a hotel. Many hotels now ban pets because of irresponsible owners. Don't bathe your Westie in the tub or use the hotel towels to dry him. If he has an accident, let the hotel know and offer to pay for rug cleaning. Always pick up after him outside, and don't let your Westie piddle right near doors or on the sidewalk. Leaving a tip for the room maids is a great idea too.

# RESOURCES

## ASSOCIATIONS AND ORGANIZATIONS

### BREED CLUBS

**American Kennel Club (AKC)**
5580 Centerview Drive
Raleigh, NC 27606
Telephone: (919) 233-9767
Fax: (919) 233-3627
E-Mail: info@akc.org
www.akc.org

**Canadian Kennel Club (CKC)**
89 Skyway Avenue, Suite 100
Etobicoke, Ontario M9W 6R4
Telephone: (416) 675-5511
Fax: (416) 675-6506
E-Mail: information@ckc.ca
www.ckc.ca

**Federation Cynologique
Internationale (FCI)**
Secretariat General de la FCI
Place Albert 1er, 13
B – 6530 Thuin
Belqique
www.fci.be

**The Kennel Club**
1 Clarges Street
London
W1J 8AB
Telephone: 0870 606 6750
Fax: 0207 518 1058
www.the-kennel-club.org.uk

**United Kennel Club (UKC)**
100 E. Kilgore Road
Kalamazoo, MI 49002-5584
Telephone: (269) 343-9020
Fax: (269) 343-7037
E-Mail: pbickell@ukcdogs.com
www.ukcdogs.com

**West Highland White Terrier Club
of America (WHWTCA)**
www.westieclubamerica.com

**The West Highland White Terrier
Club of England (WHWTCE)**
www.thewesthighland
whiteterrierclubofengland.co.uk

### PET SITTERS

**National Association of
Professional Pet Sitters**
15000 Commerce Parkway, Suite C
Mt. Laurel, New Jersey 08054
Telephone: (856) 439-0324
Fax: (856) 439-0525
E-Mail: napps@ahint.com
www.petsitters.org

**Pet Sitters International**
201 East King Street
King, NC 27021-9161
Telephone: (336) 983-9222
Fax: (336) 983-5266
E-Mail: info@petsit.com
www.petsit.com

### RESCUE ORGANIZATIONS AND ANIMAL WELFARE GROUPS

**American Humane Association
(AHA)**
63 Inverness Drive East
Englewood, CO 80112
Telephone: (303) 792-9900
Fax: 792-5333
www.americanhumane.org

**American Society for the
Prevention of Cruelty to Animals
(ASPCA)**
424 E. 92nd Street
New York, NY 10128-6804
Telephone: (212) 876-7700
www.aspca.org

**The Humane Society of the
United States (HSUS)**
2100 L Street, NW
Washington DC 20037
Telephone: (202) 452-1100
www.hsus.org

**Royal Society for the Prevention
of Cruelty to Animals (RSPCA)**
RSPCA Enquiries Service
Wilberforce Way, Southwater,
Horsham, West Sussex RH13 9RS
United Kingdom
Telephone: 0870 3335 999
Fax: 0870 7530 284
www.rspca.org.uk

### SPORTS

**International Agility Link (IAL)**
Global Administrator: Steve
Drinkwater
E-Mail: yunde@powerup.au
www.agilityclick.com/~ial

**The World Canine Freestyle
Organization, Inc.**
P.O. Box 350122
Brooklyn, NY 11235
Telephone: (718) 332-8336
Fax: (718) 646-2686
E-Mail: WCFODOGS@aol.com
www.worldcaninefreestyle.org

### THERAPY

**Delta Society**
875 124th Ave, NE, Suite 101
Bellevue, WA 98005
Telephone: (425) 679-5500
Fax: (425) 679-5539
E-Mail: info@DeltaSociety.org
www.deltasociety.org

Therapy Dogs Inc.
P.O. Box 20227
Cheyenne WY 82003
Telephone: (877) 843-7364
Fax: (307) 638-2079
E-Mail: therapydogsinc@
qwestoffice.net
www.therapydogs.com

Therapy Dogs International (TDI)
88 Bartley Road
Flanders, NJ 07836
Telephone: (973) 252-9800
Fax: (973) 252-7171
E-Mail: tdi@gti.net
www.tdi-dog.org

## TRAINING

Association of Pet Dog Trainers
(APDT)
101 North Main Street, Suite 610
Greenville, SC 29615
Telephone: (800) PET-DOGS
Fax: (864) 331-0767
E-Mail: information@apdt.com
www.apdt.com

International Association of
Animal Behavior Consultants
(IAABC)
565 Callery Road
Cranberry Township, PA 16066
E-Mail: info@iaabc.org
www.iaabc.org

National Association of Dog
Obedience Instructors (NADOI)
PMB 369
729 Grapevine Hwy.
Hurst, TX 76054-2085
www.nadoi.org

## VETERINARY AND HEALTH RESOURCES

Academy of Veterinary
Homeopathy (AVH)
P.O. Box 9280
Wilmington, DE 19809
Telephone: (866) 652-1590
Fax: (866) 652-1590
www.theavh.org

American Academy of Veterinary
Acupuncture (AAVA)
P.O. Box 1058
Glastonbury, CT 06033
Telephone: (860) 632-9911
Fax: (860) 659-8772
www.aava.org

American Animal Hospital
Association (AAHA)
12575 W. Bayaud Ave.
Lakewood, CO 80228
Telephone: (303) 986-2800
Fax: (303) 986-1700
E-Mail: info@aahanet.org
www.aahanet.org/index.cfm

American College of Veterinary
Internal Medicine (ACVIM)
1997 Wadsworth Blvd., Suite A
Lakewood, CO 80214-5293
Telephone: (800) 245-9081
Fax: (303) 231-0880
Email: ACVIM@ACVIM.org
www.acvim.org

American College of Veterinary
Ophthalmologists (ACVO)
P.O. Box 1311
Meridian, ID 83860
Telephone: (208) 466-7624
Fax: (208) 466-7693
E-Mail: office09@acvo.com
www.acvo.com

American Holistic Veterinary
Medical Association (AHVMA)
2218 Old Emmorton Road
Bel Air, MD 21015
Telephone: (410) 569-0795
Fax: (410) 569-2346
E-Mail: office@ahvma.org
www.ahvma.org

American Veterinary Medical
Association (AVMA)
1931 North Meacham Road, Suite
100
Schaumburg, IL 60173-4360
Telephone: (847) 925-8070
Fax: (847) 925-1329
E-Mail: avmainfo@avma.org
www.avma.org

ASPCA Animal Poison Control
Center
Telephone: (888) 426-4435
www.aspca.org

British Veterinary Association
(BVA)
7 Mansfield Street
London
W1G 9NQ
Telephone: 0207 636 6541
Fax: 0207 908 6349
E-Mail: bvahq@bva.co.uk
www.bva.co.uk

Canine Eye Registration
Foundation (CERF)
VMDB/CERF
1717 Philo Rd
P O Box 3007
Urbana, IL 61803-3007
Telephone: (217) 693-4800
Fax: (217) 693-4801
E-Mail: CERF@vmbd.org
www.vmdb.org

Orthopedic Foundation for
Animals (OFA)
2300 NE Nifong Blvd
Columbus, Missouri 65201-3856
Telephone: (573) 442-0418
Fax: (573) 875-5073
Email: ofa@offa.org
www.offa.org

US Food and Drug Administration
Center for Veterinary Medicine
(CVM)
7519 Standish Place
HFV-12
Rockville, MD 20855-0001
Telephone: (240) 276-9300 or (888)
INFO-FDA
http://www.fda.gov/cvm

## PUBLICATIONS
### BOOKS

Anderson, Teoti. *The Super Simple Guide to Housetraining.* Neptune City: TFH Publications, 2004.

Anne, Jonna, with Mary Straus. *The Healthy Dog Cookbook: 50 Nutritious and Delicious Recipes Your Dog Will Love.* UK: Ivy Press Limited, 2008.

Arnel, Jill. Terra-Nova *The West Highland White Terrier.* Neptune City: TFH Publications, Inc., 2006.

De Vito, Dominique. Animal Planet *West Highland White Terriers.* Neptune City: TFH Publications, Inc., 2009.

## MAGAZINES
### AKC Family Dog
American Kennel Club
260 Madison Avenue
New York, NY 10016
Telephone: (800) 490-5675
E-Mail: familydog@akc.org
www.akc.org/pubs/familydog

### AKC Gazette
American Kennel Club
260 Madison Avenue
New York, NY 10016
Telephone: (800) 533-7323
E-Mail: gazette@akc.org
www.akc.org/pubs/gazette

### Dog & Kennel
Pet Publishing, Inc.
7-L Dundas Circle
Greensboro, NC 27407
Telephone: (336) 292-4272
Fax: (336) 292-4272
E-Mail: info@petpublishing.com
www.dogandkennel.com

### Dogs Monthly
Ascot House
High Street, Ascot,
Berkshire SL5 7JG
United Kingdom
Telephone: 0870 730 8433
Fax: 0870 730 8431
E-Mail: admin@rtc-associates.freeserve.co.uk
www.corsini.co.uk/dogsmonthly

## WEBSITES
Nylabone
www.nylabone.com

TFH Publications, Inc.
www.tfh.com

# INDEX

Note: **Boldfaced** numbers indicate illustrations and sidebars.

## A

activities
    agility, 123–124
    Canine Good Citizens (program), 98, 122–123
    conformation, 124–125
    coursing ability, 125
    earthdog trials, 12, 125–126
    freestyle, 126–127
    obedience and rally, 127–128
    therapy work, 128
    tracking, 12, 128–129
acupuncture, 86
agility activities, 123–124
air travel, 131–132
allergies, inhalant, 83–84
alternative therapies, 86–87
American Kennel Club (AKC), 11
American Working Terrier Association (AWTA), 125–126
anal glands, 63
Animal Behavior Society (ABS), 119
atopy, defined, 83

## B

barking behaviors, 109–110
bathing Westies, 62–63
bedding, types of, 32–33
behaviors. *See* problem behaviors
body size/types (physical characteristic), 18–19
booster shots, 76
*Bordetella bronchiseptica,* 77–78
Boston Terriers, 15
bowls, food and water, 35–36
brushes and combs, 36, 59–60

## C

Cairn Terriers, **8**
Camcrest Bebe Queen of Trouble (famous Westie), 15
Canadian West Highland White Terrier Club (CWHWTC), 11–12, 14–15
canine adenovirus, 75
canine cognitive dysfunction (CCD), 89
Canine Good Citizen (program), 98, 122–123
canine hepatitis, 75–76
*Canis familiaris,* 6
canned foods, 50
Caras, Roger, 21
carbohydrates, value of, 44
car travel, 129–131
cataracts, 84
C. Blythfell Fergus (famous Westie), 15
certified applied animal behaviorists (CAAB), 119
characteristics
    energy levels, 24
    environment and, 24–26
    exercise requirements, 26–28
    physical appearance, 18–20
    temperament, 21–24
chewing behaviors, 110–111
*Cheyletiella,* 81
Chihuahuas, 6
chiropractic care, 86–87
chondroitin, 88
coat and skin care (physical characteristic), 19, 59
collar types, 33–34
coloration (physical characteristic), 8–9
come command, 101–102
commands, teaching, 98–102
commercial foods, 50–51
companionability, 21–24
conformation, 124–125
Conner, Daryl, **67**
copper toxicosis, 84
core vaccinations, 75–78
coursing ability, 125
cranial mandibular osteopathy (CMO), 84–85
crate training, 96–97
crate types, 34–35
Crufts (dog show), 10–11

## D

defecation (problems), 113–114
demodectic mange, 81
*Demodex,* 81
dental care, 59, 64
digging behaviors, 111–113

*Dignity and Impudence,* 8
distemper, 75–77
down command, 100–101
dry foods, 52

**E**

ears

care of, 64–65
shape of, 19–20
earthdog trials, 12, 125–126
Elfinbrook Simon (famous Westie), 15
energy levels, 24
English Kennel Club, 11
environmental adaptability, 24–26
exercise requirements, 26–28
eye care, 65–66, 84

**F**

fats, importance of, 44–45
feeding Westies
commercial foods, 50–51
    non-commerial foods, 51–53
    nutritional basics, 44–46
    obesity, 54–55
    reading labels, 47–50
    times for, 53–54
feet shape (physical characteristic), 20
first aid, 87–88
fleas, 80–81
free-feeding, 53
freestyle activities, 126–127

**G**

gates, training with, 32
glucosamine, 88
grooming Westies
    dental care, 59, 64
    ear care, 64–65
    eye care, 65–66
    finding groomers, 68–69
    as health checks, 58
    nail care, 66–68
    supplies for, 36–37, 59
guaranteed analysis of foods, 47–48
guarding behaviors, 116–119

**H**

hand-stripping, 60–62
head shape (physical characteristic), 19
health care
    alternative therapies, 86–87
    annual checkups, 73–74
    finding a vet, 72–73
    first aid, 87–88
    parasites, 79–83
    senior Westies, 88–89
    spaying and neutering, 74–75
    vaccinations, 75–78
    Westie-specific issues, 83–86
heartworms, 82–83
herbal remedies, 87
Highland Terrier, 8
holistic healing, 87
home-cooked foods, 53
hookworms, 83
Hufnagel, Carol, 15

**I**

identification for Westies, 37–39
International Association of Animal Behavior Consultants (IAABC), 119
Irish Wolfhounds, 6

**J**

joint supplements, 88
jumping behaviors, 114–116

**L**

labels for foods, 47–50
Landseer, Sir Edwin, 8
leash training, 102–104
leash types, 39
Legg-Calve-Perthes disease, 85
leptospirosis, 78–79
lodging when traveling, 132–133
lung diseases, 85–86
Lyme disease, 79, 81–82

**M**

Malcom, Edward Donald, 8–9
mange, demodectic, 81
mental exercises, 27–28
microchips, 38
minerals, importance of, 45
Miniature Schnauzers, 15
mites, 81
Montgomery Kennel Club, 13, 15
mosquito-borne diseases, 82–83

**N**

nail care, 37, 66–68
neck shape (physical characteristic), 20
nipping behaviors, 116–117
non-commercial foods, 51–53
nutritional basics, 44–46

**O**

obedience and rally activities, 127–128. See also training
obesity, 54–55
origins
    development of, 7–8
    English and American Westies, 11–14
    first Westies, 8
    history of dog, 6–7
    lineage, 9–10
    popularity of Westies, 15–16
    ranking Westies, 15
    Westie development, 7–8

**P**

Pacey, Cyril (May), 11, 15
pack hunting, 21
parasites, 79–83
parvovirus, 75, 77
patellar luxation, 85
pet-friendly lodging, 132–133
physical characteristics, 18–20
physical exercises, 26–27
Pittenweem Terriers, 9
prey drive, 28
problem behaviors
    barking, 109–110
    behavior specialists, 119
    chewing, 110–111
    digging, 111–113
    jumping, 114–116
    nipping and guarding, 116–119
    soiling, 113–114
proteins, importance of,

45–46
pulmonary fibrosis, 85–86

**R**
rabies vaccinations, 75, 77
raw foods, 52–53
resource guarding behaviors,
  116–119
ringworm, 81
Roseneath Terrier, 11
roundworms, 83
rural environments, 25

**S**
Sanders, Anne, **92**
scheduled feedings, 54
scissors, grooming, 37
Scottish Terriers, 9
semi-moist foods, 51
senior dogs, 74, 88–89
Shiningcliff Simon (famous
  Westie), 11
show dogs, 10–11
shows
  Crufts, 10–11
  Montgomery County
    Kennel Club, 15
sit command, 99–100
skin and coat care, 19, 59
socialization training, 22,
  93–96
soiling behaviors, 113–114
spaying and neutering,
  74–75
sports. See activities
stay command, 101
suburban environments, 25
supplies

crate types, 34–35
grooming, 36–37, 59
home types, 32–33
identification, 37–39
leashes, 39
toys, 39–41
Symmetra Snip (famous
  Westie), 15

**T**
tables, grooming, 36
tags, identification, 37–38
tail shape (physical
  characteristic), 20
tapeworms, 83
tattoos, as identification, 39
temperament
  (characteristic), 21–24
terriers, defined, 7–8
therapy dogs, 128
ticks, 81–82
toys, types of, 39–41
tracking activities, 12,
  128–129
training considerations
  basic commands, 98–102
  crate, 96–97
  finding trainers, 104–105
  house, 97–98
  leash, 102–104
  positive training, 92–93
  socialization, 22, 93–96
  training methods, 28–29,
    90–105
traveling with Westies,
  129–132

**U**
urban environments, 25
urination (problems), 113–114

**V**
vaccinations, 75–78
veterinarians, finding, 72–73
vitamins, importance of, 46

**W**
water, importance of, 46–47
West Highland Terriers
  (Westies)
    activities for, 120–133
    human compatibility,
      23–24
    lineage, 9–10
    national clubs, 10–14
    origins, 4–8
West Highland White
  Terrier Club of America
  (WHWTCA), 10–14
*Westie Imprint* (magazine),
  13–14
Westie lung disease, 85–86
whipworms, 83
white shaker syndrome, 86
Wolvey Pattern (famous
  Westie), 15
Wolvey Westies, 11
worms (internal), 82–83

**Y**
Yorkshire Terriers, 15

**Z**
zoonotic diseases, 77

## PHOTO CREDITS

## DEDICATION

This book is dedicated to the many Westies and Westie mixes who have made me smile over the years with their antics. Special thanks to Angus, Fred, and Charlie. To Flash, Pembroke Welsh Corgi but with many terrier-like behaviors—I suspect this will be our last book together. Many thanks for your "assistance" over the last 13 years.

## ACKNOWLEDGMENTS

I would like to thank the Westie owners and breeders who contributed their knowledge and expertise to make this book a useful and fun resource for Westie families: Lori Moffa; Pam Whittles; Daryl Conner, Master Pet Stylist; Anne Sanders of Rime Westies; Deb Waters of Aquablanca Westies; Debbie Duncan for Westie insights; and Sandy Campbell of Camcrest Westies.

## ABOUT THE AUTHOR

**Debra M. Eldredge, DVM,** is a semi-retired veterinarian and writer with many years of dog involvement. From competing in dog sports to instructing training classes in agility, obedience, rally, and grooming and handling, Dr. Eldredge has interacted with dogs of many breeds. She particularly enjoys seeing dogs do the work they were meant to do. While she currently has herding dogs, terrier fun days rank near the top of great outings! Dr. Eldredge lives on a small farm in upstate New York.

## ABOUT ANIMAL PLANET™

Animal Planet™ is the only television network dedicated exclusively to the connection between humans and animals. The network brings people of all ages together by tapping into our fundamental fascination with animals through an array of fresh programming that includes humor, competition, drama, and spectacle from the animal kingdom.

## ABOUT *DOGS 101*

The most comprehensive—and most endearing—dog encyclopedia on television, *DOGS 101* spotlights the adorable, the feisty and the unexpected. A wide-ranging rundown of everyone's favorite dog breeds—from the Dalmatian to Xoloitzcuintli —this series surveys a variety of breeds for their behavioral quirks, genetic history, most famous examples and wildest trivia. Learn which dogs are best for urban living and which would be the best fit for your family. Using a mix of animal experts, pop-culture footage and stylized dog photography, *DOGS 101* is an unprecedented look at man's best friend.